# HELP HEAL PTSD

*Healing America's Heroes:*
*Garland's Legacy*

CHUCK DENNY

Printed Worldwide
First Printing 2024
First Edition 2024

10 9 8 7 6 5 4 3 2 1

Website: HelpHealPTSD.com

ISBN: 9798324553944

# DEDICATION

This book is dedicated to **Garland B. Denny** and every single person who has helped his effort to Heal America's Heroes.

Thank you!

This story would not exist if it were not for GOD and many selfless American's who worked together with Garland to spread a message of inspiration, hope, and love for our veterans and for our country!

# TABLE OF CONTENTS


FOREWORD .................................................................. 1

INTRODUCTION ......................................................... 7

SERVING UNCLE SAM ............................................. 13

HONORABLE DISCHARGE ..................................... 21

A HISTORICAL FACT ............................................... 27

A FATHER'S REQUEST ........................................... 29

CHAW ........................................................................ 33

LOSING A SON ....................................................... 41

THE VETERANS PETITION .................................... 45

POTUS ...................................................................... 53

A DREAM UNFULFILLED ...................................... 60

CARRY ON STRONG ............................................. 66

LETTERS .................................................................. 72

PROPOSAL TO THE UNITED STATES POSTAL SERVICE ...................... 96

IMPATIENTLY WAITING ........................................ 112

A BEER ..................................................................... 116

MY TRUMP CARDS ............................................... 120

THE ALZHEIMER'S STAMP .................................. 129

NO POLITICS – JUST PATRIOTISM ...................... 131

DAD'S DREAM ON DISPLAY ................................ 141

# FOREWORD

Matthew J. Friedman MD, PhD

This book chronicles the vision, compassion, persistence, resourcefulness, and triumph of a father and son, Garland and Chuck Denny, who worked tirelessly to support efforts to find effective treatments for veterans with Post-Traumatic Stress Disorder (PTSD) and to help their families.

From campaigning on street corners, soliciting through the American Veteran Foundation (which Chuck Denny founded), lobbying congressional representatives and other elected officials, and meeting with four different presidents, this dream finally became a reality when the Healing PTSD Stamp was issued by the Postmaster General on December 2, 2019.

The basic strategy was to use a portion of the proceeds from the sale of 60 cent postage stamps, that could be purchased by any American, to develop the most effective treatments for veterans with the disorder. Of course, PTSD is not restricted to veterans so any benefits from the Stamp-Out PTSD initiative will also benefit civilian survivors of terrorist attacks (e.g. September 11th), sexual violence, domestic violence, urban violence, and natural disasters. Unfortunately, Garland, a Korean War Navy veteran, never lived to see fulfilment of his dream because he died in 2015. But Chuck saw the mission successfully completed when the Healing PTSD Stamp made its first appearance in 2019. To date, more than 18 million stamps have been sold which has raised more than two million dollars.

I first became aware of the Stamp-Out PTSD initiative more than six years ago, in December 2017, when I received an email followed by a phone call in which Chuck Denny told me that the U.S. Postal Service had accepted their proposal to create a new semi-postal stamp to raise funds to improve PTSD treatment. I was honored, humbled, and delighted when Chuck told me that the money generated by the sale of these stamps was to be donated to the Department of Veterans' Affairs (VA's) National Center for PTSD (NCPTSD) of which I had served as Executive Director since its establishment in 1989.

Let me tell you a little about PTSD. It's not just something that happens to veterans because of war zone experiences. It can happen to any man, woman or child who is in the wrong place at the wrong time. PTSD is an occupational risk for people who professionally put themselves in harm's way (such as military personnel, police, firefighters, journalists, etc.) or people who are exposed to the gruesome consequences of violence (such as emergency medical personnel, military/VA mental health personnel, disaster responders, etc.) It can occur when people are overwhelmed by catastrophic events with which they are unable to successfully cope psychologically. I'm talking about interpersonal violence such as warfare, assault, rape, terrorist attacks, and child abuse. Natural disasters such as tornadoes, hurricanes and earthquakes can also cause PTSD. Although such events happen to more than half of all American adults, they are much more common in places like Ukraine, Syria, Yemen, El Salvador, Nigeria, and other nations marked by war, civil unrest or forced migration. About 8% of all Americans have had PTSD at some point in their lives so it really is one of our most common psychiatric disorders.

I will go into some detail later on about how NCPTSD plans to use the money generated by the sale of Healing PTSD Stamps to develop very effective PTSD treatments from a precision medicine approach. But it's important for me to emphasize that although there is plenty of room for improvement, we already have some very good treatments for PTSD. Unfortunately, because of the stigma against mental illness, many people who would benefit from PTSD treatment, refuse to look for help and continue to suffer unnecessarily. I hope that anyone reading these remarks will take this to heart and seek treatment for themselves or a loved one if PTSD is affecting their lives.

Since you have a whole book ahead of you about the life of Garland Denny and the successful campaign that he and his son, Chuck, initiated to create the Healing PTSD Stamp, I'd like to tell you a little about NCPTSD. I want you to know that I played no part in the Denny's decision to entrust NCPTSD with the revenue generated by these stamps. I can only assume that they considered us the appropriate organization to fulfill their mission, to advance our understanding and treatment of PTSD, because NCPTSD has emerged as the world's leading research and educational center of excellence on PTSD and traumatic stress. Since most of you probably don't know much about NCPTSD, let me tell you a little about our research, educational and other activities. If you want to know more, you can check out our website <ptsd.va.gov>.

The National Center's extensive research program is dedicated to understanding the mechanisms by which PTSD affects behavior, emotions, cognition, and brain function. That knowledge is used to develop more effective treatments for the disorder. The National Center's research has spanned everything from investigating PTSD-related genetic or molecular abnormalities, to clinical trials to test new treatments, to finding ways to get clinicians to implement evidence-based treatments, to public health initiatives following major catastrophes such as large-scale terrorist attacks or natural disasters. We were the first to identify abnormalities in brain structure and function associated with PTSD, 30 years ago. And NCPTSD investigators have conducted some of the largest randomized clinical trials on PTSD treatment involving hundreds of veterans, military personnel, and civilians.

I must also mention our website, <ptsd.va.gov>, the biggest and best PTSD internet site in the world. In addition, our two online publications:

PTSD Research Quarterly and Clinician's Trauma Update, our many video-conferenced and online lectures, our training programs, our mobile apps, our computerized PTSD bibliographic database, PTSDpubs, (which is also the biggest and best in the world), have extended our influence to scientists, practitioners, educators, veterans, veteran families, trauma survivors and others around the world. And our Mentoring and Consultation Programs have enabled us to work directly with PTSD program directors, as well as clinicians in the trenches, making NCPTSD much more relevant and accessible to VA clinicians and, indirectly to the veterans they serve.

One of the unexpected aspects of my work at the National Center was that headlines on the morning news might force me to drop what I was doing and become my major preoccupation for the next weeks or months. We've been involved in numerous national and international crises such as the Columbine shooting, Oklahoma City bombing, Hurricane Katrina, the Balkan Wars, the September 11th attacks, the Asian tsunami, the recent wars in Iraq and Afghanistan, etc. For example, following the 9/11 attacks we worked closely with New York City and State, as well as with Federal authorities to help set up treatment programs, most notably with New York City fire fighters and first responders. Following the horrific shooting at the Sandy Hook Elementary School in Newtown, CT, we trained scores of therapists to provide treatment to pupils, families, and teachers. Throughout the wars in Iraq and Afghanistan we have worked very closely with colleagues in the US Military to establish treatment programs and to carry out research concerning returning troops. And, of course, our highest priority is to develop the best treatments and support for all VA practitioners in the trenches to help all veterans and their families overcome the symptoms and adverse consequences of PTSD.

The Center plans to use the funds generated by Healing PTSD stamp to develop and test precision medicine approaches for treating PTSD. Precision medicine customizes treatments by taking into account individual differences in gene expression, environments and lifestyles so that doctors can have a more complete understanding of a particular disease in order to select the specific treatment that is most likely to help a specific patient. All branches of medicine, these days, are searching for precision medicine treatments for everything from common illnesses such as diabetes and hypertension to rare neurological and endocrinological disorders. PTSD is no different. A key to this initiative is the Center's National PTSD Brain Bank which seeks to discover which genes are abnormally activated or suppressed among people with PTSD. Hopefully that information will, someday, help us design more effective treatments for the disorder. For example, with a precision medicine approach, two patients with PTSD may exhibit very different patterns of abnormal gerne expression and therefore, require two very different treatments to alleviate their distress. We are in a very early stage of developing precision medicine approaches for PTSD which is why the resources generated from Stamp-Out PTSD are so important and may make a significant difference.

Finally, I want to restate my gratitude to Garland and Chuck Denny for their remarkable accomplishment. I and all of my colleagues at NCPTSD will do everything we can to Help Heal PTSD and to justify the faith and confidence they have put in us.

Matthew J. Friedman MD, PhD

Emeritus Professor and Vice Chair for Research, Department of Psychiatry, Geisel School of

Medicine at Dartmouth

Emeritus (First) Executive Director, National Center for PTSD, U.S. Department of Veterans Affairs

1989-2014

Emeritus (Founding) Director, National PTSD Brain Bank, U.S Department of Veterans Affairs 2014-2022

# INTRODUCTION

Before we dive into this true American story, it is important to reiterate a portion of Dr. Friedman's comments from the Foreword; specifically, that Post-Traumatic Stress Disorder (PTSD) is real, and it will affect eight out of ten Americans in our lifetime. PTSD can affect any person, a wife, veterans, doctors, civilians, police, nurses, retirees, politicians, schoolteachers, truckdrivers, homemakers, judges, jailers, or children. There are no bounds with PTSD; it does not discriminate based on age, color, race, religion, disability, nationality, sexual orientation, or political party. PTSD has played a significant role in our family history and that is why I am sharing these stories with you. If we are ever going to destigmatize this disorder, difficult stories must be shared so we can learn and improve from them. So, I am authoring this book about my dad, our family, and the many people that we have met over the last decade who are collectively working to inspire people that may be suffering from PTSD to go seek treatment.

This is my father, his name is Garland Bram Denny, and he was born on June 6, 1931, in a log cabin on Governor Henry Carter Stuart's Farm in Elk

Garden, Virginia. The name of the farm listed on property records was The Stuart Land & Cattle Company. I am not sure if that cabin is still standing there today but there is a video of the location on YouTube if you are interested in checking the property out.

*Vaught & Martha Denny*

Garland was the second child born to Vaught and Martha Denny. He had a big brother named John Thomas, they called him "Johnny" and he was a year and a half older than him.

Shortly after Garland was born, their mother Martha became extremely ill and suddenly passed away from complications of childbirth. Garland was about 14 months old, and Vaught was not even thirty years old at this time of his life.

With two infant boys, he was fighting his way through tough times and the great depression. Vaught had to do it handicapped. Luckily, he had a close sister named Cora, and she would care for Garland and Johnny while Vaught was at work or away from home.

When he was just 10 years old, Vaught lost his right arm while he was helping his dad at work one day, that was in North Tazewell, Virginia. It was an act of God that he even survived that traumatic event. In an instant, he was pulled into the mill conveyor system and his limb was completely torn from its socket. Vaught had also broken both of his legs when he fell back to the ground.

From my understanding of his early years, life constantly challenged Pawpaw Vaught, and he questioned himself and his ability to be a great father, brother, and man. One day, Vaught told Cora to "take care of his boys." I do not believe she really understood the impact of those words on that day, Vaught was really telling her goodbye, he planned to end his life. I cannot begin to imagine his pain, or his reasoning. He had lost an arm earlier in life, now he had lost the mother of his boys. What other demons had he been battling? We all know the mind plays tricks on us and of course, the devil is always lying in wait to play his part too.

Vaught went and bought a bottle of liquor. He rolled up a drop cord, roped it over his shoulder, and started on a lonely hike into the Blue Ridge Mountains. He found a spot that was special to him, and he began to climb a tree. When he got to a limb that would hold him, he tied the drop cord around his neck and secured it to a higher branch above him. Then he began to drink away his sorrows, the color of that liquor in that bottle I will never know. As Vaught sat on that tree, he realized he was at the lowest point of his life. In that moment, GOD spoke to him, and those words went on to impact thousands of people, you will see.

*Vaught & Virginia Denny*

GOD told him to climb down from that tree and throw that liquor away because there were bigger plans for him and his family. That is what Pawpaw did. Vaught would go on to rebuild his life and heal with the help of the Lord. He started: 1. Going to church. 2. Reading his bible. 3. Having faith and believing in our Lord and Savior, Jesus Christ. Vaught went on to marry Ms. Virginia Warner, she was a schoolteacher and together they had three children, David, Charles, and Karen.

Garland loved having more siblings and he always looked forward to visiting with our "Northern" family after he moved away later in his life. There was one time when Dad told me he was taking Pawpaw Vaught on an adventure. Pawpaw wanted to take a trip back up to Saltville, Virginia. One of the last places they went to visit was that old flour mill that had removed his arm. I have a brick from the foundation of the mill sitting in my home, it serves as a reminder of what he endured. Garland swiped it when he took his dad to visit the location of the tragedy, it was a pilgrimage for them, before Vaught passed away. I am glad I have that brick and I am also glad that I know the story behind it.

We will revisit Vaught and Virginia a little later in the book because the story gets even better. Every single one of us is playing an instrumental part in the world, and we haven't yet realized how our actions might be changing the stars. Look for the smallest piece of the positive when things aren't going right in your world and run with it, most of all, believe in yourself.

Looking back at what I know about both of my elders, I learned in the toughest moments of life's situations, we should recognize that the presented difficulty is only at this moment. Have faith that this part of life is only temporary, it will change for the better if you take time to focus on healing and forgiving yourself as well as others.

# SERVING UNCLE SAM

On September 28, 1948, Garland followed in the footsteps of his big brother John and joined the US Navy. He was sent to the Naval Training Station at Great Lakes, Illinois. After bootcamp, Garland and his brother Johnny ended up serving on the *USS Roosevelt* which was stationed out of Norfolk, Virginia and they traveled to some magnificent places together.

*The Mighty USS Roosevelt*

I remember Dad telling me about navigating the Strait of Gibraltar, how he saw the Leaning Tower of Piza in Italy and he also told me stories about those Navy guys who liked JUMPING off the flight deck whenever the ship pulled into port. No chute mind you. That's a five-story free fall, he said they had to wear shoes to ease the pain when they hit the water.

On the ship, Garland worked in the boiler room. His job was to shovel coal all day to power that vessel, he literally fed the fire. He mentioned it was hotter than the flames of hell in there and the walls were lined with asbestos.

Early in my childhood, I remember dad telling me he served Uncle Sam when the ships were made of wood and the sailors were made of steel.

On November 12, 1949, the *USS Roosevelt* crossed the Artic Circle and Garland entered the Northern Domain of the Polar Bear. That earned Garland and Johnny into Ye Royal Order of "Blue Nose." They got an informal certificate, that was issued to every sailor that crossed the artic circle their first time. Look up that location on your globe.

Dad also earned another accolade during this time in the Navy. He kept the card they gave him during the adventure, I found it in a binder notebook, he had it laminated alongside proof of his honorable discharge.

You can barely see it, but his card was signed by Captain Fitzhugh Lee, and it recognized the ruler of the Dardanelles at the time, Sultan Muhammed II. It says "**<u>Danny</u>, Garland B.**" I would have never seen it in ink for myself had I not taken the time to pay attention to what is right in front of me. It's clearly "**<u>Danny</u>**", that is interesting because that is the only document I've obtained where his name is not correct, there is also a "B". Read the headline banner in the picture and ponder it. We've already spoken about Navy Jumpers too. Could these be clues that uncover some stories that haven't been told yet?

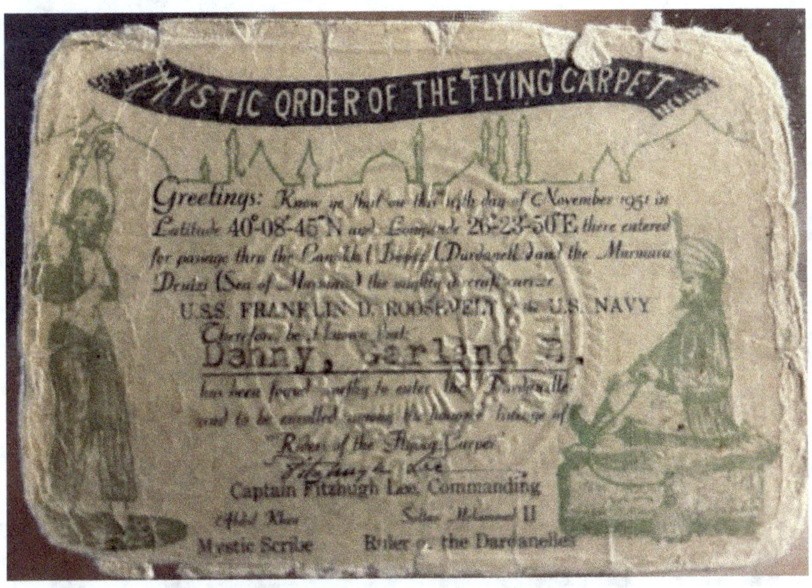


It's important to note that Garland Denny served on the *USS Roosevelt* during the Korean War. I don't know much about his younger days of service in the Navy, I am much more versed in the time he served Uncle Sam when he was not enlisted.

By my account, Dad's picture collection proves he served America for almost two decades. Before his stamp project he advocated for lower health care costs for the self-employed. He was paid by the treasury for his first four years of service, but all the others were paid on his own dime. His stint in the Navy as a younger man prepared him for a much bigger mission later in his life. Single handedly, Garland eventually brought thousands of people together from all over America to Help Heal PTSD and I'm excited to share his efforts with you.

He did it by good ole' <u>Politickin'</u>. He reached out to folks serving in all levels of government, mayors, governors, house representatives, senators, and presidents. He started calling their offices relentlessly until he got to speak with someone higher up in the staff hierarchy. Garland was the poster child of endurance and tenacity, and he never gave up on his mission – no matter what!

*Garland Denny with NC Governor Jim Hunt*

I have a great story to share about the first time he met Bill Clinton back in 1995. Governor James B. Hunt of North Carolina had a great relationship with Garland. The Governor reached out and told Dad that President Clinton was coming to town, and he asked him if he wanted to join him to greet the president at the airport when he flew into town. Of course, Dad said yes, and the events of that day really fueled dad's political fire.

I have some great pictures of that memory, here is one with Dad and the Governor chatting while they were waiting on the tarmac for Air Force One to arrive. And then here is another of Dad with President Clinton. You can see the Secret Service in the background and my father is giving the president an earful before he left to perform his duties in Charlotte for the day.

*Garland Denny with President Bill Clinton*

After the motorcade pulled away from the airport and the excitement of the moment had passed, Dad started the long walk back to his car. He had his disposable camera with him, he had all his paperwork that he showed the president, but something was missing, he had misplaced the keys to his

Plymouth. He frantically re-traced his steps, and he couldn't find them for nothing. Garland was devastated because what he was really looking to do was head right over to the photo lab to get his filmed developed.

He eventually had to flag down a State Trooper who was working at the event that day and explained his situation. Dad was a hot mess; he was so excited that he got to meet and speak with President Clinton that he was crying and visibly shaken. The Trooper was so concerned about Garland that he drove him over to our home in south Charlotte so he could get the extra key to the car and then he drove him back to the National Guard Center to get his car.

That was the second time that Garland had ever met a President in person, and it would not be his last. The first time was when he met President Gerald Ford but there was no picture. He was so excited this day because he had physical proof of the encounter; along with a few memories that would last his lifetime.

*Garland Denny with President Jimmy Carter*

President Carter was the third president my dad met in person. They met at a book signing in Charlotte, North Carolina. I know dad was there serving veterans that day, the last line on his shirt reads: www.VeteransPetition.com.

That website doesn't work any longer, but I have all the content that was put on there. I'm thinking about submitting it to the Library of Congress, along with these photos, what do you think?

# HONORABLE DISCHARGE

On September 8, 1952, Garland was honorably discharged from the US Navy. He left Norfolk and went back home to Roanoke, Virginia. I've been told that he ran a pool hall, was a little rambunctious, and went on to work in a grocery store. On November 5, 1953, he was lucky enough to walk my mother home from her high school. I know this because mama left an entry in her journal. Her name was Margaret Anne Thomas.

The thing is, my mom was already married to another man, a Navy guy, named Robert H. "Bob" Sours Jr. She had married Bob on December 20, 1952, in Roanoke. She was only 16 years old, and she was still in High School. Bob was enlisted in the Navy, and they spent a lot of time apart. She wrote in her journal "It seems like they were always saying goodbye."

There are numerous journal entries about Bob and his family in that little red book of days. The guy wrote her a few hundred letters too, many of them from the Naval Training Center in Bainbridge, Maryland. I took the time to read a lot of them, but not all of them because they seemed to be a lot of the same ole, same ole. He called her Ann, not Anne and if I had to give you a quick opinion of ole Mr. Bob (from what I read) he pretty much seemed like a narcissistic genius of his own conception. Those letters were all about him and what he was doing, which was mainly just complaining.

I remember dad telling me the story about meeting my mama and taking her to her senior high dance. Sometime after that, they were writing notes on a piece of paper to each other, and mama wrote that she would divorce Bob. Dad wrote back on the same brown piece of paper "Let's you and I get married when you get rid of him." I have that piece of paper, it's a treasure to me so I keep it with a few other important to me documents in a safe location, of course.

Mama's divorce from Bob was finalized on November 1, 1954. I have the papers to prove it. On March 5, 1955, Garland and Margaret Anne were hitched and they moved into the basement of her parent's house on 13th Street in Roanoke, Virginia. Her father, John Ralph Thomas, dug out the basement by hand so they would have their own private place to live. He installed a big window directly under the front stoop to let some natural light in, that beautiful home is still standing there today.

Dad got a job at Mick or Mac Grocery store when they were first married. The next year in late April, their first son James Thomas was born. Everyone calls him Jimmy. Martha Sue wasn't too far behind, she always likes to call herself "Dad's Favorite Daughter", she was born in 1958. At some point after their first two children were born, dad scored a job as a draftsman at US Steel. Things were working out well for them.

In 1961, Garland Scott, the couple's second son was born, and it was getting tight living in that basement. Dad had a stable income from drafting, and he had inherited some money when his next-door neighbor Mr. Kimmerling passed away. Dad used the funds to make a down payment for their first home, it was over on Rolling Hills Avenue.

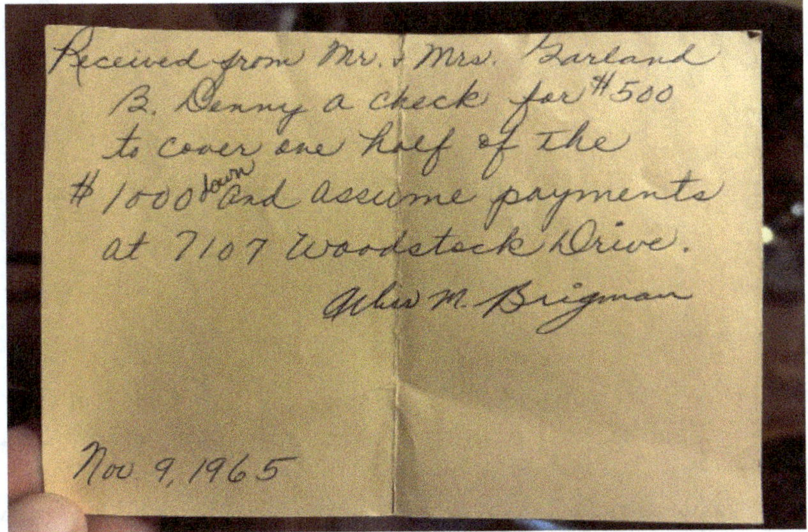



They lived happily over there for a few years and eventually Garland left his family in Roanoke for a brief period in 1965 to pursue a new business venture. He traveled down to Charlotte, North Carolina to open a structural steel drafting business with his brother Johnny. It was called Denny and Denny Inc. He was able to make enough money to put a down payment on a home in the Charlotte area so the rest of the family could move down to live with him.

On January 12, 1966, they all reunited in their new home on Woodstock Drive in Charlotte, North Carolina. And then in April of 1971, I was born into the world.

Most of my younger years are a blur to me, but thankfully we have lots of pictures that help jog my memory of that beautiful home. I was proud of that palace we lived in, but it looks a lot different these days. There was the coolest rock that sat at the front of the driveway on the left side of this photo, it held a perfect circle that my big behind could fit in, the perfect seat that I used many times during my life. Not too long ago I drove by to take another peek at our past. I was hoping to see mama's favorite elephant ears still planted in the front bed or to catch a glimpse of the peonies, rosebushes, or the hydrangeas that we had planted over the years. She has been kept up well, but she doesn't look the same, the rock is missing too.

They say the only thing constant in our life is change, and I am good with that.

Memory lane quickly reminded me of the cool features around that area, there was a large creek right down the hill by our home, it's called Sugar Creek, it is part of the Mecklenburg Greenway now but back in the old days we called it Huntingtowne Park.

There is a long foot bridge over it, and it is encased by a chain link fence to keep you from falling in; dad would take me there sometimes in the afternoons to shoot my bb gun. He had just as much fun as I did, we would aim for the turtles as they surfaced from the stinky water. He told me to rest the gun on the fence and I would be a better aim. Quickly afterward he told me when I hit them with the bb not to worry, we could never hurt them, and they wouldn't hold it against us. I can see him smile at me now as I write this story.

That home and the time I spent with my parents and my brother Scotty hold a lot of memories for me. We would still see Jimmy and Sue regularly, but it was the 4 of us and the three dogs most of the time. I can remember hanging out just belly laughing about many of the antics that went on around there. Most of the time we were downstairs in the den, or out in the backyard.

There used to be a red and white fire alarm in front of our house, it was posted on the telephone pole at the end of our driveway. It was 911 before 911 existed and many someone's pulled it a couple of times when I was a kid.

We spent hours playing frisbee in the road and throwing baseballs and footballs in the front yard. Sledding down Watercrest Drive in the winter were some of the best memories. When we came back inside to thaw out, mama's homemade veggie soup was always waiting for us in a pot on the stove. Garland set us up on the Southside of Charlotte pretty well, it was the perfect place to grow up as a kid.

# A HISTORICAL FACT

You might find this information a bit random for this book, but I hope you will look beyond that. There was a historic event that happened in 1971. It was traumatic for the people involved; I am sure.

In November of that year, Flight #305 out of Portland was hijacked by a nice man in his 40's who told the stewardess that had a bomb after the flight had taken off. The plane was persuaded to land because he demanded a $200,000 ransom and 4 parachutes to release his hostages. The plane took flight again with instructions to head towards Mexico and at some point, the man jumped from the rear steps of the plane. His identity is still unproven to this day. Additionally, this is the longest standing **UNSOLVED** case in the FBI's history.

Now, in case you are wondering, I am not saying this event is related to Garland at all but the timing of it related to my birthyear and the subject manner led me to include it here for reference.

Here is a link to the details of the case:

https://www.fbi.gov/history/famous-cases/db-cooper-hijacking

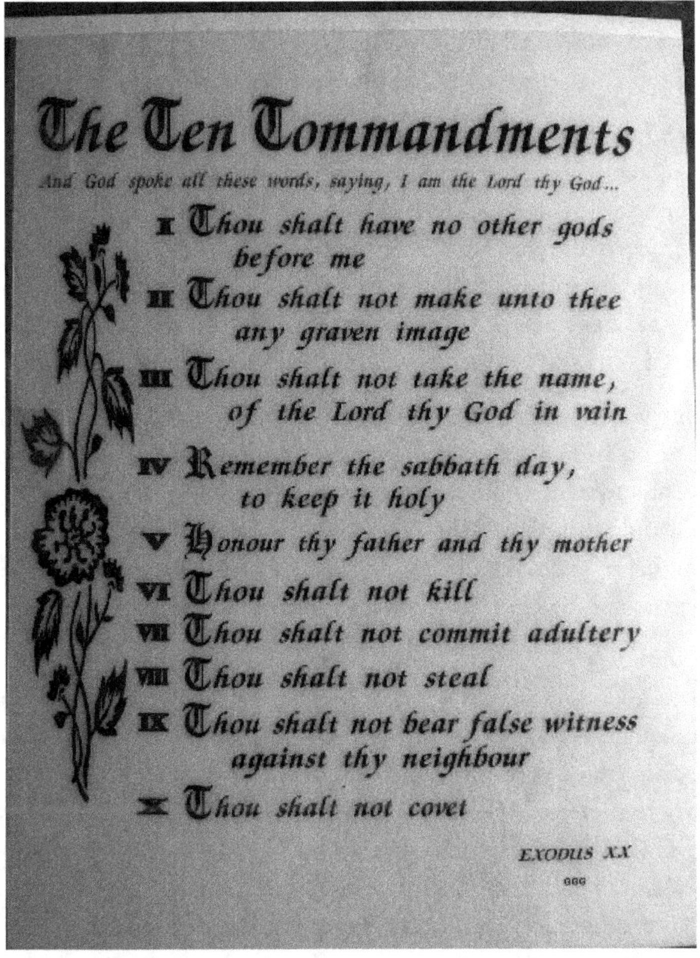



Pawpaw Vaught was a quiet man. He was gentle, loving and kind to me in every memory. He was very soft spoken, and I loved that WCW Wrestling was always on the tv Saturday afternoon's when we visited. Every time I saw my pawpaw, he was wearing a button-down dress shirt with slacks and perfectly shined dress shoes; the sleeve where his arm was missing, was always tucked into his waist.

Usually, we would drive up to Roanoke every Easter and Thanksgiving. There was a cherry tree and a grape vine in pawpaw's backyard, and I loved plucking off those cherries the most. Granny's green bean casserole, homemade apples and a little turkey and dressing helped to calm my sugar rush. I can still smell the food cooking in the kitchen and hear that grandfather clock ringing throughout their house in my mind right now.

I told you the story earlier about GOD speaking to my pawpaw while he was in a tree and how that changed the course of his life. What I didn't mention was how he spent his time from those days forward. Vaught's mission became to get The Ten Commandments back into churches and schools. Oddly enough, aside from the bible, you don't see GOD's main rules posted anywhere in these places. Pawpaw was going to change that, and he did it by sharing the story of how he was saved.

After his wife Virginia suddenly passed away, Vaught recognized that his ability to push that initiative ahead was slowly coming to an end. So, he asked Garland if he would do what he could do to see that more places and people would display GOD's rules. Garland told his father that he would carry on his mission. And from the 1990's on, dad spent more of his time in churches and coming up with a plan to meet his father's request.

Sometime after 2003, Garland started making prints of The Ten Commandments and the 23rd Psalm. He created many different designs, he would laminate them and then put them in a nice frame. He would visit churches and donate the prints to them if they would simply post them somewhere they could be seen. He then decided to visit schools, and local businesses too. There are many places he visited here near our home that obliged him, I smile every time I see one. I knew he was the one that had it placed there because he marked them at the bottom with this symbol "GGG". That stood for "GOD Gives Grace" it was penned by Garland, Gillespie and Guy. He had some success but as we all know religion is a touchy subject, so his efforts faced challenges along the way as well.

One Christmas season, dad leased a kiosk at the mall during Christmas in Monroe, NC. He would spend his days talking with people about GOD and how we should be better people. He made some sales but not enough to recoup his investment, but he was ok with that, he was carrying on his father's request.

I am honored to include their work together here; it was a long time in the making. I was proud of my dad standing in the way of adversity during those years, I didn't recognize it as much back then as I do today. One of the many positive aspects of those times was that Garland got a chance to meet with a lot of veterans and his encounters inspired him to serve in a new way. He put his promise and future mission to our entire family, and we all helped him how we could along the way.

This is one of the last pictures we took of our family together. It was taken at a time when GOD was challenging us all and I cherish this moment that was captured, now more than ever.

Dad and Pawpaw Vaught taught our family some huge lessons that were challenging to understand at times. It was that GOD has a plan for us all if we will simply open our hearts and listen to him. You must take chances to show your faith especially when there is no clear path forward.

Ask GOD for forgiveness for your sins. Take more time to love & forgive your family, AND MOST OF ALL FORGIVE YOURSELF.

Believe that your future holds happiness - no matter how hard the times are right now. These are not statements said to minimize your struggle, they're meant to encourage your recovery.

# CHAW

Garland worked hard and he played hard too. He would normally leave his office around 4pm and on the way home he loved to visit one of his favorite beer joints. It was a ritual for him. The top three were "The Hule'" pronounced who-lee, "Diamond Point" which was at a bend in the road and "The Cobber" that was the coolest place of them all because you had to have a special card just to get in the door. Plus, they had a shuffleboard. These were all little dive bars up on South Boulevard in Charlotte and only one of them remains operating today. Dad loved people, he loved pool, he loved golf, and gambling a little bit too.

These places were almost like second homes to me when I was young. We would walk in and go to the bar; he would order a Miller Lite and I would get a Coke on ice in a cocktail glass. Then dad would hand me a stack of quarters and tell me to go play pinball. I'd drag over a barstool to the machine; I'd climb up in the chair and have a blast. The Kiss pinball machine was one of my favorites. I thought their makeup, the music and the artwork were fascinating.

As far back as I can recall, dad was a cigarette smoker, he was a moderate drinker, and he loved chaw. There were always foil pouches of Redman Chewing Tobacco laying around his office and on the table beside his recliner at our home. Day's Work Plug was a popular choice for him too. He had this antique ceramic spittoon that sat on the hearth of our fireplace on Woodstock Drive. The sights and smells that thing produced were disgusting but I still have that treasure. It's all dried out now and it has suffered a little battle damage over the course of time too. I don't think I have ever spit into it once so maybe it's time to try something new.

*Garland Denny at The Hule'*

That reminds me of one Saturday morning when we were driving in a green Plymouth Reliant up through Fancy Gap. It is a treacherously beautiful stretch of I-77 in Virginia. We were on the way to Roanoke, and I remember dad keeping his eyes on the road as he reached down looking for his water cup, but he ended up grabbing his spit cup and he took a big swig from it. Mama and I started laughing as he quickly pulled off the side of the road to hurl. If that won't make someone quit chewing chaw, I don't know what would, lol.

Let's fast forward to a morning in 1981, mom and I went down to the hospital with dad because he had to have an in-patient test done. He had been suffering from heartburn and shortness of breath a lot and mama convinced him to go see the doctor and thankfully that doctor ordered this test. They took him into the surgery room, and he was fully awake during the procedure. They inserted a needle into an artery near his groin and then pumped some kind of dye into him so they could see the condition of his arteries. He watched it in real time on the monitor with the staff.

Within a few moments of laying on that operating table, dad's life changed forever. They told him he had 3 arteries that were blocked with calcium.

Two were blocked over 90% and the other was in the high 70% range. He was 50 years old when he found this out and I was 10. The doctors eventually decided to treat him with medication, and they told him his habits and his diet needed to change.

Growing up, all I remember eating was red meat and pork. We never had fish, or chicken. We ate pot roast on most Sundays, it had taters, carrots and a big onion that were all soaked in mama's delicious brown gravy. Spaghetti with meat sauce and shit-on-a-shingle were our other regular meals. That is creamed chipped beef on toast in case you are wondering, and this dinner menu was all about to change because the doctor said so!

Dad quit smoking and chewing cold turkey. He started eating veggie plates at his favorite lunch diners. There were to be no more hotdogs at Andy & Greg's place and no more Mr. K. Burgers. Man, I miss those places today. Mama wanted to make sure dad stayed healthy at dinnertime too, so she went to The Little Professor bookstore at Park Road Shopping Center and bought a book called "365 Different Ways to Cook Chicken", I still have that book today.

Dad cut back on drinking cold beer, that was never much of a problem for him anyway. He was the kind of man that could drink two beers and walk away. I always admired that he had that ability. He took a liking to one glass of wine, every now again, but he really put in the effort to improve his health. He said he did it for his wife and his kids. As it turns out, those decisions went on to help thousands of people that he never even knew.

As we grew older, he never said so, but I could tell that he felt like a ticking time bomb. Can you imagine hearing that about your heart and then the doctor says, "Don't worry, here are a few pills." The good news is, this strategy worked pretty good up until 2009, that's when Dad had triple by-pass surgery along with a heart valve replacement at the same time.

He was 78 years old and under a ton of stress. My mama had developed dementia by this time, he was caring for her and all their animals around the house too. It was like a farm but not really. There was Sweetie Pie, he was a meaner than hell teacup poodle that tore dad's hand open so bad one time that he needed stitches, but he didn't get them. They had Buddy the one-eyed cat. They had another cat named Hattie Bell who lived in the garage. Mama also had two birds, Willie was a Blue Crowned Conjure and Barney was a quaker. Aside from all the daily chores dad was also working on his Veteran's Petition project in full force.

All those moments had caught up to him and he asked my sister Sue to drive him to the hospital because he was having heart trouble, he knew something was wrong and they didn't want to wait on the ambulance to get there. They got my dad down to the Emergency Room at Presbyterian Hospital on 7th Street. He was stabilized and the next morning he was scheduled to have surgery.

He asked us all to leave the hospital for the night and come back in the morning before he went down for the procedure. The thing is the hospital staff surprised him that next morning; they came earlier than expected to prepare him for surgery. It sent dad into a tizzy because he had it in his mind, he would see us and there was no way they were going to wheel him into ICU without him getting the chance to pray with his family, which includes the Reverend Thomas Gillespie.

We all got there in time to be with dad, and Rev. Tom led our prayer over him and I'm glad we did. As they rolled dad down to surgery, he passed away on the gurney outside of the operating room. Luckily, they were on the way to put him on life support for the surgery anyway and the quick-thinking hospital staff had already saved his life before starting the surgery.

*Chuck Denny with Rev. Tom Gillespie*

He was in the operating room for what seemed like an eternity, and we didn't find out that part of the story until he was in the recovery room. Doctor Chan came out and told us that dad made it out of surgery, but he still had some concerns and he also explained to us what happened prior to the surgery outside of the operating room. And now, for some unknown reason he was continuing to lose blood and that was puzzling to them. We asked if we could go in and see him, and he said yes.

As we stood over our father, Doctor Chan went on to tell us that dad had to have numerous blood transfusions in the recovery room. He said at some point we may have to go back in and perform a second open heart surgery on the same day. We all kissed dad on the forehead, said another little prayer and we left the ICU. The doctor came out shortly after our meeting and said they had made the decision to "go back in". This was one of the longest days of our lives.

After numerous hours, Doctor Chan returned with a smile on his face. When they reopened his chest cavity, they found what the problem was, it was with the heart valve they replaced. It needed additional sutures, as dad's heart pumped blood, the blood would leak from the valve where it wasn't completely secured. Garland would go on to make a full recovery from 2 open heart surgeries in one day, but he would need lots of rest and that my friends is something that man was never used to, resting.

As dad recovered, he went on to tell us that he heard the entire conversation as we were standing over him with Doctor Chan. He told us what was said, and he followed it up with he wasn't worried about it a bit because GOD had spoken with him to and he told him that everything would be ok, and it was! I get chills every time I tell this story, even today.

Here is a copy of Garland's medical bill for this procedure. He saved it in a binder with his veteran work, he wanted it to be shared. He was extremely thankful for the medical staff and their phenomenal work that day, but the cost, he couldn't comprehend. It leads me to remind you again of Garland's mission. He wanted our veterans to have better healthcare than the members of our congress. That shouldn't be hard for us to change in the immediate future; with many of our service members returning home from war and conflict from all over the globe, I am sure you can understand.

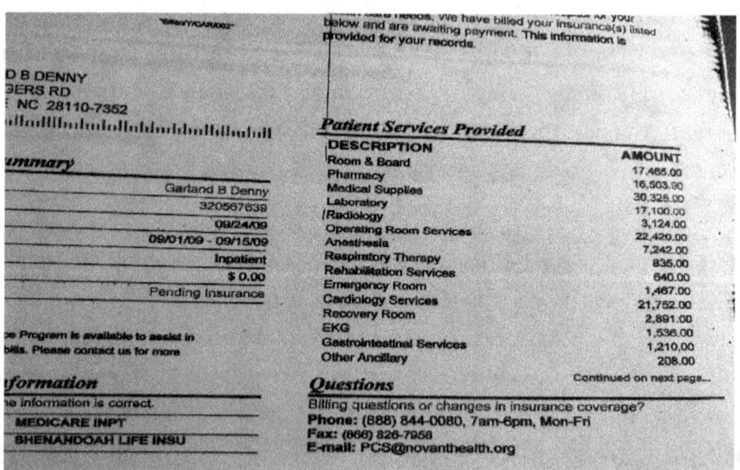

Patient Services Provided

| DESCRIPTION | AMOUNT |
| --- | --- |
| Room & Board | 17,465.00 |
| Pharmacy | 16,503.90 |
| Medical Supplies | 30,325.00 |
| Laboratory | 17,100.00 |
| Radiology | 3,124.00 |
| Operating Room Services | 22,420.00 |
| Anesthesia | 7,242.00 |
| Respiratory Therapy | 835.00 |
| Rehabilitation Services | 640.00 |
| Emergency Room | 1,467.00 |
| Cardiology Services | 21,752.00 |
| Recovery Room | 2,891.00 |
| EKG | 1,536.00 |
| Gastrointestinal Services | 1,210.00 |
| Other Ancillary | 208.00 |
| | Continued on next page... |

Questions

Billing questions or changes in insurance coverage?
Phone: (888) 844-0080, 7am-6pm, Mon-Fri
Fax: (866) 826-7958
E-mail: PCS@novanthealth.org

Here is the total billed for a Veteran of the Korean War. Two heart surgeries in one day of September of 2009. Notice in the first picture two insurance policies were used to cover it.

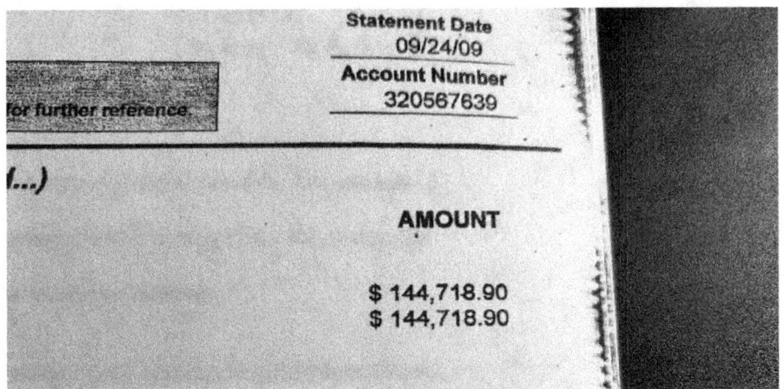


Here are two questions for all those folks up in the Capitol to ponder:

1. What would a member of Congress have to pay for the same surgery?
2. What should a veteran have to pay?

Write in your comments, what would you say to Congress?

(Use blue ink).

# LOSING A SON

On July 14, 1997, my parents got the news no parent <u>EVER</u> wants to receive, their son, Garland Scott, had passed away unexpectedly late in the evening the night before. He was found motionless on the floor of his hotel bathroom in Detroit, Michigan. He was 36 years old. I'll get to the rest of that traumatic story in a few moments but let me tell you a little bit about him.

In the late 1970's dad was heavily involved in a youth sports program in our community on the southside of Charlotte, it was called The Starclaire Athletic Association. My dad, along with a few others from the Optimist Club, had organized a football, basketball, baseball, and cheerleading program for all the kids living around our community. We have many pictures of Scotty playing football, basketball, and baseball. The organization carried on for many years and the schools around always gave them permission to use their facilities.

Many of the parents would coach their kid on a team and often they loved it so much that when their kids got too old to play, they would still be involved in the program. It helped the younger members of the community build social confidence and all the kids knew of each other back then, that's just how it worked out.

When Scotty got into high school, he developed a fondness for cigarettes, fast cars, beer, and cannabis too. He was the kind of guy that never went looking for trouble but for some reason or another it would always find him. I could write an entire book on Scotty alone, he was hilarious, and the ladies loved him too. The thing to focus on at this moment is his relationship with my father. They were best buddies and it hurt both of my parents to the core when they learned of his fate in that hotel room.

Scotty had a laugh bigger than Texas and a heart made of gold. He had a tattoo of a black panther on one shoulder and an eagle on the other inscribed with the letters "GAR".

He was a fighter that wouldn't back down when it came to what he thought was right. I remember many instances where he came home battered and bruised. Sometimes it happened because of his own making, other times he tested authority and he also had numerous car wrecks too.

He almost died in one of those wrecks which a few years prior to his death when he was traveling on his way back to Charlotte through London, Kentucky. He lost control of the car he was driving, and he was extremely intoxicated. He was thrown from the vehicle during the final impact with 2 different 18 wheelers and the hospital workers told my parents that probably helped to save his life. It was a miracle he survived; it also left him with a huge scar. It went from the lower middle of his back all the way over his shoulder, the wreck literally split him in half. He took time to heal himself physically and spiritually and went on to score a traveling job. That was how he ended up in Michigan.

After we got the news of his death my brother Jimmy flew to Detroit to identify Scotty in the morgue. Scotty's official cause of death was listed as an overdose. Even though that is what the papers say, I don't believe that is the case, not for a minute. I believe he was murdered, that is my opinion.

Scotty was up there working with the electrical union on some project. The day's work was over and like always, he was looking for a good time. The story is Scotty met a lady friend at the hotel bar and brought her back up to the room. They were hanging out with his co-worker/roommate and then Scotty and the lady decided they needed some privacy, so they stepped into the bathroom.

The coworker, who I don't believe was involved, decided to get on the telephone. After a few moments, the coworker saw the lady leave the bathroom and hurry out the door. About 15 minutes later than that, he checked on Scotty in the bathroom and found him dead on the floor. There was a needle dangling from his arm, I was told it contained heroin.

I knew my brother well enough to know he wasn't scared of any man, but a needle that was a different story. My belief is that this was an intentional act, and it was intended to hurt my father and my family. Why? I believe my dad knew why and I believe he left the answers where they would be found in the future. But for now, the remainder of this story will be left untold.

*Garland Scott Denny*

Before I wrote this story, I reached out to the Detroit Police Department with a Freedom of Information Act request regarding the death of my brother. More than 100 days have passed since I made that request and I have not been contacted by the legal team or anyone from the police department at all.

# THE VETERANS PETITION

This was where Garland focused his efforts in the last years of his life. He always wore a shirt that held his name, his VFW POST, and his website on the left side of his chest. You'll see it on his shirt in most of the pictures throughout this book. That's unspoken proof that he held this mission close to his heart.

As I sit here and remember his mentality at this time of his life, he was hyper- focused on making this dream happen. He developed a determined mindset that this project would succeed. Looking back, I realize his strong intentions to see this through may have held some hidden or undiscovered meanings too.

Garland retired in 2006 after 50 years of working on some of the largest structural steel projects in the southeast. In 2007, he founded a Veterans Petition and spent years lobbying US Presidents, Members of Congress, Governors, Mayors, and Citizens across America.

His vision was to "Put Veterans First" by bringing people together to raise money to help Veterans living with Post-Traumatic Stress Disorder. This project could be funded through the production of US Postal Stamps, Commemorative Coins and US Savings Bonds that could be sold to the public.

He considered these projects the highest calling of his career, always saying he was trying to "leave this world in a better place" after he was gone. During his lifetime, he personally met with Presidents Gerald Ford, Jimmy Carter, Bill Clinton, and Barack Obama. He has also met many members of Congress; ultimately gaining the ears of over 155 members who contacted the US Postmaster General Meghan Brennan.

*Chuck Denny, Martha Sue Tucker, and Jim Denny*

Mr. Denny was a life member of the Veterans of Foreign Wars Post 5464 in Monroe, NC. To honor his service, the Post was renamed the Garland B. Denny Memorial Post, and he was also a member of the American Legion and the Disabled American Veterans.

Garland organized a petition drive. He started off by collecting names in notebooks. He would stand on street corners, attend trade shows, and would approach anyone who came within an arm's length of him. As his support grew, I helped him build a website where his progress could be viewed and referenced online. He continued to collect names in person and from visitors over his website, but he decided to eventually focus on getting resolutions from city and county governments that represented larger populations of supporters. He started contacting Politicians, City Officials and Business Leaders. Anyone he could think of, he would reach out and ask for their support in helping Veterans. As time went on, he began receiving requests for interviews and articles relating to his Veterans project. They followed the progress of his effort in the Charlotte area for the rest of his life.

North Carolina Congressman Robert Pittenger(R) was one of Dad's biggest supporters in making this dream come true. His entire staff jumped behind Garland's efforts, especially Robert Becker and Mr. Stephen Billy. They always took dad's phone calls; they pushed forward even when there were no answers.

I can tell you dad got hundreds of Proclamations in support of his efforts, he organized them in a binder, and I put them online. It put pressure on everyone else to jump on board or look like a huge idiot. And there were a few idiots, but I'm willing to bet they will support our veterans in the end.

In November of 2013, my mom passed away. Her dementia had grown into a full case of Alzheimer's. She spent the last year of her life living in a recliner in the family room of their home. She couldn't walk, she could only muster up enough strength to stand up from the recliner and take one step to sit back down on her potty chair. That became an unbreakable routine. This broke my dad's heart, but it did not hinder his spirit to continue to love her and complete his mission.

The following year, with the help of Congressman Pittenger's staff, we scored a visit to the White House to meet with White House officials. It was not a personal meeting with President Obama, but it was a huge start in the right direction. We met with Koby Langley from the President's staff and two staffers from Congress, Mr. Stephen Billy representing the House and Mr. Robert Espinosa representing the Senate, we met in the Eisenhower Executive Office Building. Talking about a beautiful place, in the meeting room we saw the war eagle statue of General Douglas McCarther, it was a Friday, and it was my dad's 83rd birthday. A total dream for a hard-working veteran came true.

That day we learned that the main problem in pushing this forward was, President George W. Bush privatized the Post Office back in his term. So, the Executive Branch was limited; they would help but it was the US Postmaster's call if this was ever going to happen. The USPS said if this was ever going to happen it had to be an act of Congress. Congress then said, no it must come from the Postmaster. It was a stalemate that none of the smartest people in politics or government service could figure out. I mean that with all due respect.

Graciously, Mr. Billy and Mr. Langley organized a tour of the White House for us the following day. For all of dad's hard work and effort we got a personal tour of the West Wing. Dad was on top of the world that day, my wife, and my son were allowed to come with us. There were three generations of Denny's standing together in the White House. We saw the situation room, we stood in the doorway of the Oval Office just a few feet away from the resolute desk, we walked around the Cabinet room, and we hung out under that famous painting of Teddy Roosevelt on horseback in the Roosevelt room. You always see that art on tv.

One of the best moments for me was when we strolled along the Promenade and stopped right outside the Oval Office. The thought hit me that we were in one of the most romantic places we could be in America, so I snuck a kiss from my wife as we were looking at the Rose Garden. The Truman balcony was to the left, high above us. That sugar was so good I did it again downstairs in the Press Room right in front of the White House podium. I was able to document that one! It is an amazing feeling to stand in the center of the most powerful piece of real estate in the world.

Overall, we had a great trip to Washington that weekend, before we left town, we went back a second time to visit Arlington Cemetery. Dad wanted to; visit the Tomb of the Unknown Soldier, walk along the Amphitheatre, observe Audie Murphy's grave, and pray over President John F. Kennedy. I remember staring at that that eternal flame and wondering why such a good man had to die so young.

We toured Robert E. Lee's homestead and watched a funeral procession from afar. That day, we wanted to honor ALL of those that had given their lives for our freedom. It's truly a humbling experience and I believe if you call yourself an American, you should go do the same. Even if you have already been, go honor them ALL, again!

*Garland right after his West Wing Tour*

As we were driving back home to Monroe, North Carolina I know dad was a proud American. It picked up his spirit after mom had passed. When he got back settled into his home, he started making his phone calls and rounds again. He finally felt like some progress on this project was being made. I did too.

# POTUS

In August of 2014, the American Legion National Convention was held in uptown Charlotte. President Obama was invited to speak, and our friend Koby Langley put my dad and I on the official White House guest list. It was an awesome follow up to our meeting back in June. I was totally surprised when Koby reached out to me and asked if we would like to attend.

We had to be there a few hours before 1pm. I went and picked up dad at his house, he only lived a mile away from me and we rode downtown and followed the instructions we were given. When we got to the check-in area, we were required to present our identification and then go through some metal detectors before we could be issued our White House Passes.

When we got off the elevators, I snapped this picture of a sign at the entryway that said, Invited Guests Entrance". When we got into the convention room, I texted Koby and told him we were there. He came out and talked to us a few moments and then he made sure that Garland had a front row center seat to see the President speech. Since I was not a veteran, I chose to stand in the back where I would not be in anyone's way. The large room was dark, there were delegate banners everywhere that held the names of the different states.

*Garland Denny and President Barack Obama*

The North Carolina delegation was not directly in front of the presidential podium, it was another state. Once my dad scored the seat he was given, he didn't move. As the legionaries started to fill the seats around him, there was one gentleman who became a little irritated that my dad got the front row center seat. In a commanding tone, he told my father he would have to move because he was not part of that state's delegation. My dad preceded to tell the kind man that he wasn't going to budge, and "there wasn't a damn thing he was going to do about it", the man said, "oh yeah" and my dad said, "oh yeah, because I am on order to sit here by the President of the United States". Not only did my dad stand his ground with that man, but he also shook hands and spoke with the president right in front of the guy before I took this picture of them together.

Dad had another great day politickin'. It was a lot for me to take in, almost surreal. Things were moving faster now thanks to some help from many friends of veterans. After all his hard work, I was glad to see the fruits of his labor paying dividends. Dad told me on the way home that day "If you don't try, you won't succeed. Have some patience, things will come around." He sure was right.

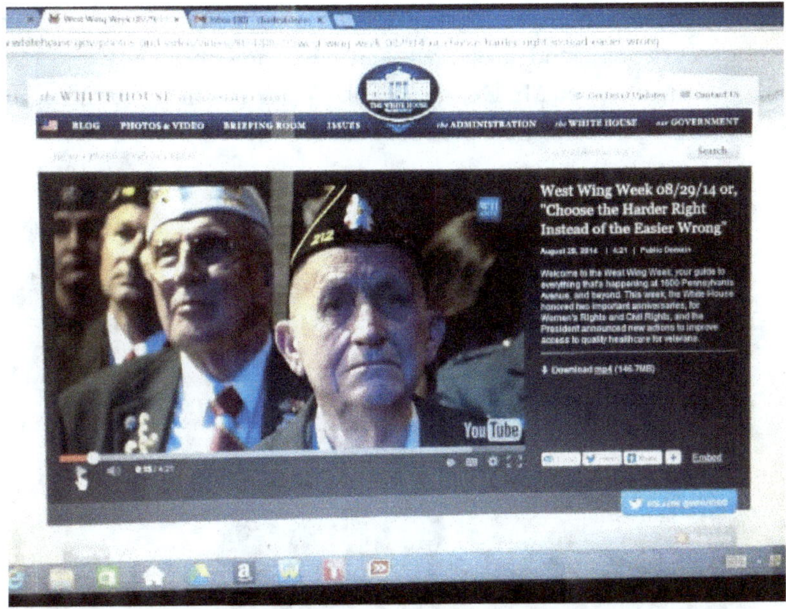

This is one of my favorite parts of this story to tell because the next day on the landing page of the White House website, there was a photo that was posted of Garland that was taken by the White House Press core from the stage. He was sitting in the front row, and you could see that kindhearted gentleman he had the friendly exchange with sitting right behind him. Dad was surrounded by veterans that he was trying to serve and only a few of them new his real intention of being there. He was there to attract the president's attention to serving our veterans with PTSD, that was his business. The fact he got to meet him and see his speech firsthand was a bonus.

The story gets even better because that was not the only time that we met with President Obama. On April 15, 2015, we got invited to see the president speak again in a more intimate setting. He held a town hall at the ImaginOn: The Joe and Joan Martin Center in uptown Charlotte. There were only a few hundred people invited to attend, and once again my dad and I had the chance to meet with President Obama and speak with him, this time a little longer.

Then an amazing sequence of events unfolded. After he completed his speech, the President made his way down from the podium to meet with the closest attendees and shake their hand. He came to my dad and I and he said I remember you Mr. Denny, "thank you for coming to see me again" and then out of nowhere, the president handed my dad a small coin.

It was a presidential challenge coin, and you can only get those from the hand of a president. My dad thanked him and said, "I have something for you too sir" and he handed him two copies of the photo you saw of them on an earlier page. The president thanked my father and asked him to wait a while so that he could finish meeting the other guests.

It was a cool moment, one of the other attendees saw the entire exchange and he came over to tell us how awesome that really was, his name was Garry McFadden, and he was on private security detail for the event. He told my father, "That is a pretty special item sir, not everyone gets one of those, look it up!" As I am writing this, Garry is currently the Mecklenburg County Sheriff, in North Carolina.

After about 20 minutes or so, one of the president's aides came back to my father and I holding one of the photos. President Obama had signed one of the photos for my dad, and overall, the day's events along with these items serve an awesome reminder to me of people working together to serve our veterans and citizens.

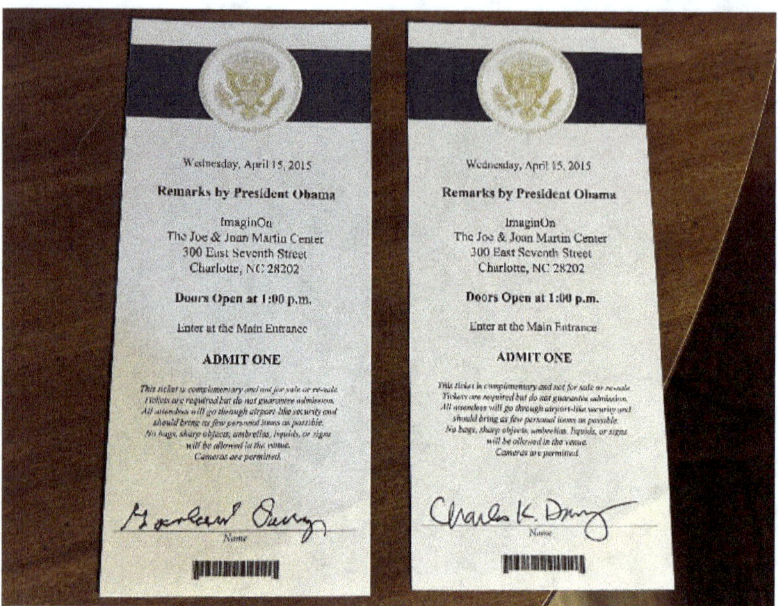

At this moment in time, we both felt like there was no stopping it now. This fueled dad's fire to get more of Congress on board, and plus it gave him some awesome bragging rights to all his family and veteran friends.

# A DREAM UNFULFILLED

nd then one morning, I went to a fast-food restaurant to pick up some breakfast for dad. It was around 8:30am and like I always did, I called him to see if he needed anything else before I headed his way. The phone rang and then the machine answered, so I said, "Dad I'm heading your way." Most of the time, he would pick up the phone right after the machine cut on because he was in the middle of something else but not today.

I pulled down the driveway, got out of my car and went over to the code pad to open his garage. I walked inside and called out to him, and he didn't answer back. As I made my way into his room, I found out why. Dad's heart had given out on him, and GOD had called him home.

I knew at this point I was too late to help him, I felt the artery at his neck to see if he had a pulse, but I knew he was already gone, he was cold and blue. I was in a trance but was composed enough to pick up his cordless phone to call 911. I told the operator that I found him unresponsive, and I described his condition and that it looked like he had been that way for a while. She told me that an officer and the lifesaving crew were on their way, so I hung up the phone and went to open the front door bawling my eyes out. Luckily, I knew they were less than 1 mile away.

An officer was the first to arrive and he asked me a few questions as I let him inside, I told him where to find my dad and that I was going to wait outside. After a few moments, I went ahead and called my siblings and by this time the firefighters were arriving. I walked back inside with them, and we talked to the officer. They all agreed that there wasn't anything that could be done, it looked like he had been there for a while so at this point, we waited for the coroner to arrive.

That happened on October 13, 2015. The memory of that event is shocking for me to talk about today. I have vivid recollections of that morning; and a firm belief that my dad passed away around 4:00am. I say that because most mornings I wake up at that time automatically. Dad visits me in my dreams often and life isn't the same without him, that is for sure. He had such a huge personality, and he could relate to anyone he met.

We had a very dynamic relationship, and if you knew Garland you know what I am talking about. The best way I could explain it is, we are both very passionate people who love to argue our point. Sometimes that could come about in an insensitive tone. He always told me to say what I mean because that's what he was going to do. He felt you should be able to do that with everyone no matter how difficult the situation, and one should accept the complications of the matter and move on without holding a grudge. I realize now, he was always feeding his fire just like the Navy taught him to do. He knew his time here on earth was limited and his plotted destination was far away, but still I had trouble understanding his impatience and demanding ways. Our whole family tried our best to get him to relax a little and he wasn't going to hear it.

After we held his funeral, things pretty much became a blur for me. It was such a beautiful event given the circumstances. We were surrounded by our family and friends and many, many veterans who were an important part of dad's life, especially over the last 8 years. This is a picture that someone snapped for us of his funeral procession. My sister was one of my dad's most trusted confidants and she was riding on the back of that second motorcycle.

*Both Photos Courtesy of KCNPhoto.com*

At the cemetery, we held a short graveside service right outside the mausoleum where my parents are interred beside their son Scotty and my great aunt Monnie. The Honor Guard with VFW Post #2423 honored Garland with a 21-gun salute, and two members of the US Navy presented our family with the American flag.

The very first veteran you see holding the flag is PFC James Crump. He stormed the beaches of Normandy. He became friends with my father when he was a member of Indian Trail Post #2423. I was honored that he was among the many men who were there to comfort our family at such a difficult time.

About 30 days after dad passed away, and just like clockwork, we got a letter from Wells Fargo Home loans. Dad had taken out a reverse mortgage to help cover the expenses of his and my mother's medication and he also used a portion of the funds to help market his Veterans project.

The big city bankers advised us that his estate had a $65,000 balance that was due in a very short time and if not paid soon, they planned to foreclose on his home. The home was worth about $200,000 at that time, and they really didn't give a damn that we had barely just gotten him into his crypt.

Thankfully, my wife is a gracious woman, and she loaned my siblings and I the money to pay off the bank before that could happen. We paid her back when we sold that home on Rogers Road in Monroe. That place was where

Garland Denny's dream to help veterans was started and without her help in this story it would never have been able to generate all the positivity that's been created thus far.

Thank you, Vanessa!

# CARRY ON STRONG

About a week after Garland passed away, he was honored on the House floor by Congressman Robert Pittenger (pictured), a Republican (NC-09). The Congressman invited us up to Washington to the House chamber to hear him speak about my dad. It was pretty cool, we met with him in his office for a short time, he presented us with a flag that was flown over the Capitol in honor of our dad and then we walked through the underground tunnel together over to the House Chamber.

While we were there in Washington, I was contacted by a White House aide and asked to stop by the White House because President Obama had written a condolence letter to me. That will be included in this chapter for you to review. Even crazier, Hillary Clinton also wrote me a condolence letter, that I received in the mail.

*Hillary Clinton, Garland Denny and Chuck Denny*

Over the years, Dad met Bill and Hillary numerous times at political events in the Charlotte area. He knew their Chiefs of Staff and he called and shared his opinions every chance he could do it. It is my belief that more people should make the effort to reach out to the House and Senate in D.C., I have seen how effective it can be firsthand.

*Garland Denny and Senator Elizabeth Dole*

I know this may be starting to sound like a snowflake sandwich to many of you, but you should understand that my dad was heavily involved with all politicians both Democrat and Republican. Here is a picture of him and Elizabeth Dole to prove it to you!

He knew that the political parties didn't matter when it came to working for our veterans. Eventually, 155 members of Congress wrote a letter to the US Postmaster General in support of dad's hard work. You'll see that letter soon. There was no Act of Congress, but there is proof in this book that "party" can be put aside to tackle tough issues. We still have some more work to do!

After such a humble experience from our leaders in Washington, I knew that it was up to **Garland's Army** to finish this task. A lot of people had come together to support him and his efforts over the years. We couldn't just quit because he passed away. Dad had spoken with me candidly up until his death, I knew his conversations and frustrations. I had an insight on making this dream a reality that others didn't have, & I knew everyone would back my efforts to continue because they all loved that man and what he was doing for veterans.

So, we banded together, everyone had a small part to play, and Garland recognized they would play it! Veterans, The VFW, The American Legion, Wounded Warrior, The VFW Ladies Auxiliary too! All my family pitched in to help too, some made phone calls, and some sent emails. Tommy Achenbach, my nephew, he helped me with research and writing important facts about PTSD that you will see in the proposal.

Our friends and associates used Facebook to spread the message, local businesses, The Carolina Panthers, and other non-profits wrote letters of support, political staffers worked hard to help too. We all fought and clawed our way to making this dream a reality. It started with a few letters you'll see in a bit and almost instantly the US Postmaster General, Meghan Brennan, she decided to join our fight too!

Americans and the government were working together to complete Garland's mission for our veterans, and I hate that he wasn't here to see the result. It took a few more months before the USPS could implement their changes to accept proposals, but they sure did, and we were on our way!

Eventually, on June 19, 2016, which was Father's Day. I sat down at my computer in a ten-by-ten bedroom on Genesis Drive and with my wife, her father and our son present, we submitted a full proposal to the Citizens Stamp Review Board over the internet. If a stamp was going to happen, things had to start with them. So, we took our shot!

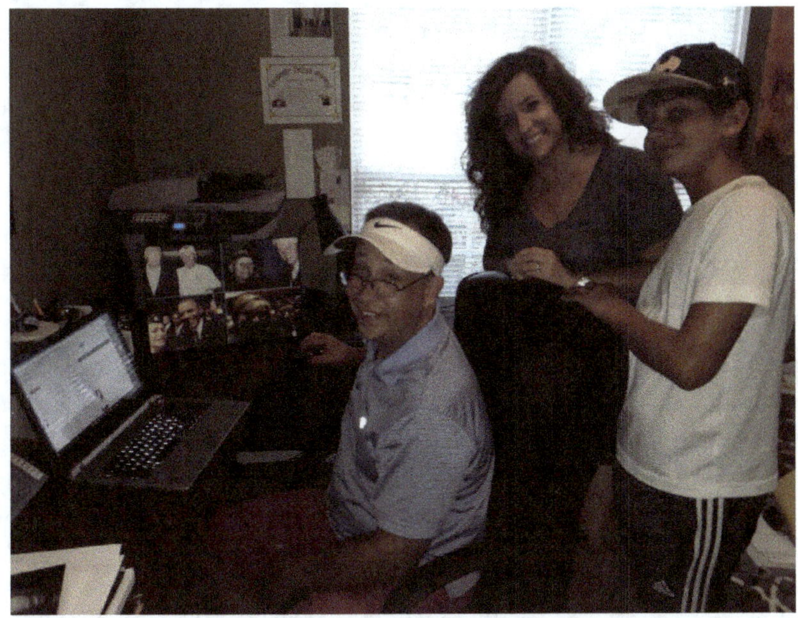

You have read some of the content I included in the proposal already, but additionally there is a whole lot more and I made sure they saw every document that was procured, every signature that was signed, all the emails, and every photo; and I was prouder than hell to realize the stars were aligning. The hearts of some great Americans had come together to change the future for our veterans and that started with Garland's dream.

If I didn't share this story with you, this journey would be buried in time. And I don't think that is right. America seems unsteady these days and we need to pull it back together. Working to help our veterans is our common ground. Now more than ever we need to see that some of the system works, especially if it is for the right cause. That's why this story is important, and I hope that you will spread the message to others so that this fire may never die. Our veterans deserve everything we can give them, and their families do too.

 Since printing costs are so high, it's not prudent for me to include all the content from the proposal in this book. But I plan to give you enough to inspire you to help us get Congress to Act! Soon you will learn how you can do your small part right from your home. I hope you will continue reading first-hand how this project got unknown folks to rally for our veterans in unison. Hopefully, this will fill your heart with more patriotism for our great land. We need to come together as a nation, and it all starts from right where you are sitting.

On the next few pages, I wanted to include some cool letters I have received over the years. They were part of this story too and it's amazing to see it all here together, written out.

Then you are going to see the conclusion of the submission that we sent to the USPS. I know I've shared a part of it already, but the rest will give you the idea on how things played out; along with real proof of why The United States of America is the best country in the world to live in. We literally wrote thousands of letters to make it happen, that is why a stamp is a great revenue generator, it is not a thing of the past.

I'm going to encourage you to write a few letters of your own later in the book. Your voice should be heard, and I hope that you will use it!

# LETTERS

*Above: Letters to Congress – Below: NC Congressman Robert Pittenger*

# Congress of the United States
## Washington, DC 20515

June 29, 2015

The Honorable Megan J. Brennan
Postmaster General
United States Postal Service
Washington, D.C.


Dear Ms. Brennan:

For nearly a decade, Mr. Garland Denny, a U.S. Navy veteran, has tirelessly worked to advocate for those who have served our Nation with courage and valor. As Members of the U.S. Senate and House of Representatives, we support Mr. Denny's call for a "Stamp out PTSD" semipostal stamp to honor America's veterans. Through increased funding for Posttraumatic Stress Disorder (PTSD) research and treatment in the U.S. Department of Veterans Affairs (VA) we can better serve our nation's heroes. With June being recognized as National PTSD Awareness Month, it is a most appropriate time for the United States Postal Service to take action to benefit the brave men and women who have served in our nation's military.

The USPS has printed and sold various semipostal stamps raising tens of millions of dollars for causes important to every American, which previously were mandated by Congress. In just three years, the Heroes of 2001 stamp raised over ten million dollars to assist the families of emergency workers who lost their lives in the line of duty during the terror attacks on September 11, 2001. The Breast Cancer Awareness stamp, first issued nearly two decades ago, has raised over eighty million dollars to fund critical research, and the Save Vanishing Species stamp has raised over two million dollars since its inception.

As you are aware, the USPS has full authority under the Semipostal Authorization Act of 2000 (P.L. 106-253) to "issue and sell semipostals under this section in order to advance such causes as the Postal Service considers to be in the national public interest and appropriate." In February 2005, the House Oversight and Government Reform Committee revised its rules and will no longer consider new semipostal stamps, given the USPS has full authority over these matters. However, in a rule issued by the USPS in 2001, the USPS has decided it will not utilize this authority until the end of the Breast Cancer Awareness stamp sales period.

The intent of this rule was to prevent an influx of semipostal stamps in the market being created by both Congress and the USPS, but the USPS has not revised the 2001 rule since Congress has officially stopped mandating new semipostal stamps.

As of today, there are currently two semipostal stamps available through the USPS; the Breast Cancer Awareness stamp, and the Save Vanishing Species stamp. Congress will no longer issue new semipostal stamps, and the USPS has previously sold three semipostal stamps simultaneously and with great success. We urge you to amend the 2001 rule pertaining to semipostal stamps and promptly begin consideration of a stamp to honor America's veterans. The proceeds of the "Stamp out PTSD" semipostal stamp should be directed to PTSD programs within the U.S. Department of Veterans Affairs (VA).

According to the VA, up to twenty percent of veterans who served in Operations Iraqi Freedom and Enduring Freedom experience PTSD. For those who served in Desert Storm, roughly twelve percent experience PTSD, and the number increases drastically for our Vietnam Veterans. The creation of the "Stamp out PTSD" semipostal stamp, which will benefit our Nation's veterans, is certainly "in the national public interest and appropriate."

We look forward to working closely with you in this effort to support the brave men and women who served our Nation and laid such a costly sacrifice upon the altar of freedom.

Thank-you.

Sincerely,

Robert Pittenger
Member of Congress

Thom Tillis
U.S. Senator

Richard Burr
U.S. Senator

Richard Hudson
Member of Congress

Alma Adams
Member of Congress

Gary Peters
United States Senator

Steve Knight
MEMBER OF CONGRESS

Blake Farenthold
MEMBER OF CONGRESS

Ryan Zinke
MEMBER OF CONGRESS

Walter Jones
MEMBER OF CONGRESS

John Culberson
MEMBER OF CONGRESS

John Shimkus
MEMBER OF CONGRESS

Earl "Buddy" Carter
MEMBER OF CONGRESS

Mark Pocan
MEMBER OF CONGRESS

Sean Patrick Maloney
MEMBER OF CONGRESS

George Holding
MEMBER OF CONGRESS

Sanford D. Bishop, Jr.
MEMBER OF CONGRESS

David Rouzer
MEMBER OF CONGRESS

Patrick Tiberi
MEMBER OF CONGRESS

Phil Roe
MEMBER OF CONGRESS

Renee Ellmers
MEMBER OF CONGRESS

Dan Newhouse
MEMBER OF CONGRESS

Peter King
MEMBER OF CONGRESS

Charles Boustany, Jr.
MEMBER OF CONGRESS

Bradley Byrne
MEMBER OF CONGRESS

Mo Brooks
MEMBER OF CONGRESS

Bill Posey
MEMBER OF CONGRESS

Ryan Costello
MEMBER OF CONGRESS

Mark Walker
MEMBER OF CONGRESS

Bill Johnson
MEMBER OF CONGRESS

Frank Guinta
MEMBER OF CONGRESS

Mike Bishop
MEMBER OF CONGRESS

Marlin Stutzman
MEMBER OF CONGRESS

J. Randy Forbes
MEMBER OF CONGRESS

Steve King
MEMBER OF CONGRESS

Rod Blum
MEMBER OF CONGRESS

John Conyers, Jr.
MEMBER OF CONGRESS

Tim Murphy
MEMBER OF CONGRESS

Gregorio Sablan
MEMBER OF CONGRESS

Cathy McMorris Rodgers
MEMBER OF CONGRESS

Randy Neugebauer
MEMBER OF CONGRESS

Todd Rokita
MEMBER OF CONGRESS

Charles Rangel
MEMBER OF CONGRESS

Pete Sessions
MEMBER OF CONGRESS

Madeleine Z. Bordallo
MEMBER OF CONGRESS

Joyce Beatty
MEMBER OF CONGRESS

Bill Huizenga
MEMBER OF CONGRESS

Marsha Blackburn
MEMBER OF CONGRESS

Brett Guthrie
MEMBER OF CONGRESS

Kristi Noem
MEMBER OF CONGRESS

Sheila Jackson Lee
MEMBER OF CONGRESS

Doug LaMalfa
MEMBER OF CONGRESS

Chris Gibson
MEMBER OF CONGRESS

Lynn Jenkins
MEMBER OF CONGRESS

Doug Lamborn
MEMBER OF CONGRESS

Joe Wilson
MEMBER OF CONGRESS

**THE WHITE HOUSE**

WASHINGTON

October 20, 2015

Mr. Charles Denny
Washington, D.C.

Dear Chuck:

I was saddened to learn of the passing of your father, Garland Denny, and I extend my heartfelt condolences as you mourn his loss.

The security that lets us live in peace, the prosperity that allows us to pursue our dreams, the freedom that we cherish—these were earned by the service and sacrifice of our Nation's veterans. We are forever indebted to these heroes, and I hope you find solace in knowing Garland's legacy lives on not only in the family and friends he left behind, but also in the country he helped defend.

At this difficult time, I hope cherished memories help temper your grief. Please know you are in my thoughts and prayers.

Sincerely,

# HILLARY RODHAM CLINTON

November 4, 2015


Mr. Charles K. Denny
2301 Genesis Drive
Monroe, NC 28110

Dear Mr. Denny:

Please accept my heartfelt condolences on the loss of your beloved father, Garland B. Denny. I was grateful to learn about the remarkable work he undertook to help his fellow veterans.

At this difficult time, please know that my thoughts and prayers are with you, your family, and all those whose lives he touched, particularly those of our brave veterans he was so devoted to helping. Your father was loved by many, and he will be greatly missed.

With deepest sympathy, I am

Sincerely yours,

Hillary Rodham Clinton

December 1, 2015

The Honorable Megan J. Brennan
Postmaster General
United States Postal Service
Washington, DC

Dear Ms. Brennan,

In June of this year, 56 members of Congress wrote a letter to you in support of my father's tireless call to "Stamp Out Ptsd" for Veterans. I have included a copy for your quick reference.

From what I understand, the USPS has amended it's rules with regard to semi-postals and you have decided not to pursue new candidates until the Breast Cancer Awareness Stamp expires in December of 2015.

I would like to ask you to consider my father's effort for a new semi postal stamp to be issued for Veterans in 2016. He passed away October 13, 2015 and he spent years generating public support for this effort. He may have gone about this outside of the guidelines of the Postal Service but it was because he was a man on a mission to help Veterans. He didn't want the fate of this project to lay in the hands of small committee because he personally met thousands of Americans who cared & felt like more needed to be done for Veterans!

He understood that the needs of our Veterans are underserved because he lived within the system. He would also say that this isn't any attempt to downplay the VA at all, it is merely an attempt to put Veterans first. The Breast Cancer Awareness Stamp generated more than $80 million in revenue, think of what we could do for Veterans! What if we put our heads together to make this even more successful than the Breast Cancer Stamp?

I was hoping you would grant me a personal meeting soon so that I may share with you my father's efforts, the stamp design and the support he generated for the last nine years. I am available at your convenience, thank you for the consideration.

Regards,

Chuck Denny
2301 Genesis Drive
Monroe, North Carolina 28110
980-721-2663

www.VeteransPetition.com

April 26, 2016

Chuck Denny
2301 Genesis Drive
Monroe, NC  28110

Dear Mr. Denny:

Thank you for your letter to the Postmaster General expressing your support for the issuance of a semipostal stamp for PTSD awareness and research.  As the Director, Stamp Services, I am responding on her behalf.

On April 20, 2016, the US Postal Service published it final rule regarding the Semipostal Stamp discretionary program.  As per this rule, we will begin accepting complete proposals for stamp subject requests beginning on May 20, 2016.  Stamp subject proposals submitted prior to May 20, 2016 will not be given consideration, but proposals may be resubmitted under the newly published regulations.  Proposals must meet all submission requirements in order to be considered.

The Federal Register notice outlining this program can be found at the following url: https://www.gpo.gov/fdsys/pkg/FR-2016-04-20/pdf/2016-09081.pdf

Thank you for your interest in our stamp program.

Sincerely,

Mary-Anne Penner
Director, Stamp Services

# Congress of the United States
## Washington, DC 20515

May 20, 2016

The Honorable Megan J. Brennan
Postmaster General
United States Postal Service
Washington D.C.

Dear Ms. Brennan:

As Senators and Members of Congress, we applaud the United States Postal Service's recent rule change to allow for the production of new semipostal stamps, and fully support the semipostal stamp submission of Charles Denny, the StampOut PTSD stamp.

A semipostal stamp is required to maintain broad national appeal, and support a national public interest furthering human welfare. The StampOut PTSD stamp submission states the stamp proceeds will be directed to the research and treatment of PTSD effecting our military veterans, with an emphasis on treatment.

According to the U.S. Veterans Administration, up to twenty percent of veterans who served in Operations Iraqi Freedom and Enduring Freedom experience PTSD. Twelve percent of veterans who served in Desert Storm suffer from PTSD, and that number increases drastically for our Vietnam veterans.

The men and women who serve in our military sacrifice much in the cause to protect the United States and stand for the liberties which are the foundation of our nation. We should honor their sacrifice through a national showing of support, and through utilizing this alternative funding mechanism to increase treatment for veterans suffering from PTSD.

Mr. Garland Denny, a veteran himself, worked tirelessly for nearly a decade in an effort to support increased care for veterans before passing away last year. With his son Charles carrying the torch for his father, we urge the USPS to select the StampOut PTSD stamp as the first semipostal stamp under the new discretionary program.

We look forward to working with the USPS throughout the selection process, and to helping make the StampOut PTSD stamp an enormous success.

Sincerely,

Richard Burr
Senator

Thom Tillis
Senator

Robert Pittenger
Member of Congress

Jan Schakowsky
MEMBER OF CONGRESS

Beto O'Rourke
MEMBER OF CONGRESS

Scott DesJarlais
MEMBER OF CONGRESS

Daniel Kildee
MEMBER OF CONGRESS

Sanford D. Bishop, Jr.
MEMBER OF CONGRESS

Jeff Denham
MEMBER OF CONGRESS

Garret Graves
MEMBER OF CONGRESS

Austin Scott
MEMBER OF CONGRESS

Walter Jones
MEMBER OF CONGRESS

Ann Wagner
MEMBER OF CONGRESS

John K. Delaney
MEMBER OF CONGRESS

Chris Smith
MEMBER OF CONGRESS

David Joyce
MEMBER OF CONGRESS

Trent Franks
MEMBER OF CONGRESS

Robert Aderholt
MEMBER OF CONGRESS

Michael Capuano
MEMBER OF CONGRESS

Frank Guinta
MEMBER OF CONGRESS

David Young
MEMBER OF CONGRESS

Rodney Davis
MEMBER OF CONGRESS

Stephen Fincher
MEMBER OF CONGRESS

Kevin Cramer
MEMBER OF CONGRESS

Frank Lucas
MEMBER OF CONGRESS

Randy Neugebauer
MEMBER OF CONGRESS

Bruce Poliquin
MEMBER OF CONGRESS

Jackie Walorski
MEMBER OF CONGRESS

Jeff Fortenberry
MEMBER OF CONGRESS

Al Green
MEMBER OF CONGRESS

Michael McCaul
MEMBER OF CONGRESS

Barbara Comstock
MEMBER OF CONGRESS

Richard Hudson
MEMBER OF CONGRESS

Sean Duffy
MEMBER OF CONGRESS

Marcy Kaptur
MEMBER OF CONGRESS

Bill Huizenga
MEMBER OF CONGRESS

John Shimkus
MEMBER OF CONGRESS

David B. McKinley
MEMBER OF CONGRESS

Susan W. Brooks
MEMBER OF CONGRESS

Stephen Lynch
MEMBER OF CONGRESS

Pete Aguilar
MEMBER OF CONGRESS

Pete Olson
MEMBER OF CONGRESS

Ron DeSantis
MEMBER OF CONGRESS

Bill Johnson
MEMBER OF CONGRESS

Dana Rohrabacher
MEMBER OF CONGRESS

Carlos Curbelo
MEMBER OF CONGRESS

Will B. Hurd
MEMBER OF CONGRESS

Joe Kennedy
MEMBER OF CONGRESS

Tom Rice
MEMBER OF CONGRESS

Chris P. Gibson
MEMBER OF CONGRESS

Adam Kinzinger
MEMBER OF CONGRESS

Peter T. King
MEMBER OF CONGRESS

Dave Brat
MEMBER OF CONGRESS

Raúl R. Labrador
MEMBER OF CONGRESS

Darrell Issa
MEMBER OF CONGRESS

Lynn Westmoreland
MEMBER OF CONGRESS

Mario Diaz-Balart
MEMBER OF CONGRESS

Gus Bilirakis
MEMBER OF CONGRESS

Tim Walberg
MEMBER OF CONGRESS

George Holding
MEMBER OF CONGRESS

David Scott
MEMBER OF CONGRESS

Steve Stivers
MEMBER OF CONGRESS

Marsha Blackburn
MEMBER OF CONGRESS

Ken Calvert
MEMBER OF CONGRESS

Tulsi Gabbard
MEMBER OF CONGRESS

Steve Knight
MEMBER OF CONGRESS

Tim Ryan
MEMBER OF CONGRESS

Walter Jones
MEMBER OF CONGRESS

Diane Black
MEMBER OF CONGRESS

Andre Carson
MEMBER OF CONGRESS

David Rouzer
MEMBER OF CONGRESS

French Hill
MEMBER OF CONGRESS

Dan Benishek
MEMBER OF CONGRESS

Mike Conaway
MEMBER OF CONGRESS

Earl L. Buddy Carter
MEMBER OF CONGRESS

Todd Rokita
MEMBER OF CONGRESS

Mike Rogers
MEMBER OF CONGRESS

Henry Cuellar
MEMBER OF CONGRESS

Lynn Jenkins
MEMBER OF CONGRESS

Bob Goodlatte
MEMBER OF CONGRESS

Pat Roberts
SENATOR

Bill Flores
MEMBER OF CONGRESS

Hank Johnson
MEMBER OF CONGRESS

Alan Lowenthal
MEMBER OF CONGRESS

Keith Ellison
MEMBER OF CONGRESS

Brenda Lawrence
MEMBER OF CONGRESS

Ralph Abraham
MEMBER OF CONGRESS

David G. Valadao
MEMBER OF CONGRESS

Paul Cook
MEMBER OF CONGRESS

David N. Cicilline
MEMBER OF CONGRESS

John Katko
MEMBER OF CONGRESS

Steve Pearce
MEMBER OF CONGRESS

Sean Patrick Maloney
MEMBER OF CONGRESS

William R. Keating
MEMBER OF CONGRESS

Chris Gibson
MEMBER OF CONGRESS

Brad Ashford
MEMBER OF CONGRESS

Mike Honda
MEMBER OF CONGRESS

G. K. Butterfield
MEMBER OF CONGRESS

Bradley Byrne
MEMBER OF CONGRESS

Mike Kelly
MEMBER OF CONGRESS

Rob Blum
MEMBER OF CONGRESS

Alma Adams
MEMBER OF CONGRESS

Sam Graves
MEMBER OF CONGRESS

Tony Cárdenas
MEMBER OF CONGRESS

John Moolenaar
MEMBER OF CONGRESS

Darin LaHood
MEMBER OF CONGRESS

Randy Hultgren
MEMBER OF CONGRESS

Larry Bucshon
MEMBER OF CONGRESS

Joseph Pitts
MEMBER OF CONGRESS

Chuck Fleischmann
MEMBER OF CONGRESS

Doug LaMalfa
MEMBER OF CONGRESS

Rob Woodall
MEMBER OF CONGRESS

Mike Bost
MEMBER OF CONGRESS

Scott Tipton
MEMBER OF CONGRESS

William Lacy Clay
MEMBER OF CONGRESS

Lois Frankel
MEMBER OF CONGRESS

Roger Williams
MEMBER OF CONGRESS

Ted Deutch
MEMBER OF CONGRESS

John Shimkus
MEMBER OF CONGRESS

Kay Granger
MEMBER OF CONGRESS

Glenn Thompson
MEMBER OF CONGRESS

Janice Hahn
MEMBER OF CONGRESS

John Fleming
MEMBER OF CONGRESS

Adam Schiff
MEMBER OF CONGRESS

Debbie Wasserman Schultz
MEMBER OF CONGRESS

John Mica
MEMBER OF CONGRESS

Blaine Luetkemeyer
MEMBER OF CONGRESS

Linda T. Sánchez
MEMBER OF CONGRESS

Luis Gutiérrez
MEMBER OF CONGRESS

Kyrsten Sinema
MEMBER OF CONGRESS

Kristi Noem
MEMBER OF CONGRESS

**THE SECRETARY OF VETERANS AFFAIRS**
**WASHINGTON**

June 7, 2016

The Honorable Megan J. Brennan
Postmaster General
United States Postal Service
Washington, DC  20260

Dear Ms. Brennan:

The Department of Veterans Affairs (VA), an executive agency as defined by 5 U.S.C. 105, supports the proposal to establish a stamp under the United States Postal Service's Semi-Postal Discretionary Program to support the education, research and treatment of posttraumatic stress disorder for U.S. military Veterans.

VA has the desire and ability to implement the proposal and accedes to the Semi-Postal Authorization Act's requirements for reporting to Congress the amounts received under the program and reporting the total amount of the funding received each fiscal year, further describing the significant advances or accomplishments funded out of those amounts.

Thank you for your support of our Nation's Veterans.

Sincerely,

Robert A. McDonald

# PROPOSAL TO THE UNITED STATES POSTAL SERVICE

## Semi-Postal Discretionary Program

June 19, 2016

"Stamp Out PTSD" for Veterans

<u>We, The People</u> will show that America cares!

TO: <u>Office of Stamp Services</u>

Attn: Semipostal Discretionary Program

475 L'Enfant Plaza SW., Room 3300

<u>Washington, DC 20260-3501</u>

<u>semipostal@usps.gov</u> – email

From: <u>Garland B. Denny</u>

Attn: Charles K. Denny 2301 Genesis Drive

Monroe, North Carolina 28110

The Recipient Executive Agency:

The United States Department of Veterans Affairs (VA)

In the supporting documents section of this proposal, you will find a letter from the VA stating it is an Executive Agency as defined in 5 U.S.C. 105. It was signed by the Secretary of Veterans Affairs, Robert McDonald stating they are willing and able to implement this proposal for Veterans. You will also notice in his letter they state they are willing and able to meet the requirements of the Semi-postal Authorization Act, should this proposal be selected.

## Purposes for which these funds will be used:

In order to afford the public a convenient way to contribute to funding for Post-Traumatic Stress Disorder (PTSD) research and treatment of U.S.

military veterans, the Postal Service shall establish a special rate of postage for first-class mail pursuant to current Semi-postal stamps.

Of the amounts becoming available for PTSD research and treatment of U.S. military veterans pursuant to this stamp, the Postal Service shall pay 100 percent to the U.S. Department of Veterans Affairs (the Department), with those funds becoming available to the National Center for PTSD or other applicable agencies within the Department for PTSD education, research, and treatment of U.S. military veterans, with an emphasis on treatment.

Payments under this paragraph to an agency shall be made under such arrangements as the Postal Service shall by mutual agreement with such agency establish in order to carry out the purposes of this submission, except that, under those arrangements, payments to such agency shall be made at least twice a year. An agency that receives amounts from the Postal Service under this paragraph shall use the amounts for Post-Traumatic Stress disorder education, research, and treatment of U.S. military veterans.

These funds should not directly or indirectly cause a net decrease in total funds received by the Department of Veterans Affairs below the level that would otherwise have been received but for the enactment of creation of this stamp.

# Benefiting the National Public Interest

# & Furthering Human Welfare

## I. Veterans are the nucleus of our nation!

nucleus - the central and most important part of an object, movement, or group, forming the basis for its activity and growth.

Without their sacrifice & commitment to uphold the Constitution of the United States, our country would not exist today! Taking our time to identify & address the medical needs of those who volunteer to serve is not only in our national public interest, but it should also be our highest national priority!

On June 25, 2015, the United States Senate Passed a Resolution (S.RES 215) designating the month of June 2015 as "National Post-Traumatic Stress Disorder Awareness Month" and June 27,2015 as "National Post-Traumatic Stress Disorder Awareness Day".

This resolution outlines many reasons to focus on serving Veterans living with Post Traumatic Stress. The US Senate felt compelled to address the issue of PTSD, so I find it fitting to include their resolution here.

Whereas the brave men and women of the Armed Forces of the United States, who proudly serve the United States, risk their lives to protect the freedom of the people of the United States, and deserve the investment of every possible resource to ensure their lasting physical, mental, and emotional well-being.

Whereas more than 2,000,000 members of the Armed Forces have deployed overseas since the events of September 11, 2001, and have served in places such as Afghanistan and Iraq.

Whereas the Armed Forces of the United States have sustained a historically high operational tempo since September 11, 2001, with many members of the Armed Forces deploying overseas multiple times, placing those members at high risk of post-traumatic stress disorder (referred to in this preamble as "PTSD").

Whereas men and women of the Armed Forces and veterans who served before September 11, 2001, remain at risk for PTSD and other mental health disorders.

Whereas the Secretary of Veterans Affairs reports that—

(1) since October 2001, more than 390,000 of the approximately

1,160,000 veterans of Operation Enduring Freedom, Operation Iraqi Freedom, and Operation New Dawn who have received health care from the Department of Veterans Affairs have been diagnosed with PTSD.

(2)in fiscal year 2014, more than 531,000 of the nearly 6,000,000 veterans who sought care at a medical facility of the Department of Veterans Affairs received treatment for PTSD; and

(3)of veterans who served in Operation Enduring Freedom, Operation Iraqi Freedom, and Operation New Dawn who are receiving health care from the Department of Veterans Affairs, more than 615,000 have received a diagnosis for at least 1 mental health disorder.

Whereas many cases of PTSD remain unreported, undiagnosed, and untreated due to a lack of awareness about PTSD and the persistent stigma associated with mental health conditions.

Whereas exposure to military trauma can lead to PTSD.

Whereas PTSD significantly increases the risk of anxiety, depression, suicide, homelessness, and drug- and alcohol-related disorders and deaths, especially if left untreated.

Whereas public perceptions of PTSD or other mental health disorders create unique challenges for veterans seeking employment.

Whereas the Department of Defense and the Department of Veterans Affairs—as well as the larger medical community, both private and public—have made significant advances in the identification, prevention, diagnosis, and treatment of PTSD and the symptoms of PTSD, but many challenges remain.

Whereas increased understanding of PTSD can help diminish the stigma attached to this mental health issue, and additional efforts are needed to find further ways to reduce this stigma—including an examination of how PTSD is discussed in the United States and a recognition that PTSD is a common injury that is treatable and repairable.

Whereas PTSD can result from any number of stressors other than combat, including rape, sexual assault, battery, torture, confinement, child abuse, car accidents, train wrecks, plane crashes, bombings, or natural disaster, and affects approximately 8,000,000 adults in the United States annually; and Whereas the designation of a National Post-Traumatic Stress Disorder Awareness Month and a National Post-Traumatic Stress Disorder Day will raise public awareness about issues related to PTSD, reduce the stigma associated with PTSD, and help ensure that those suffering from the invisible wounds of war receive proper treatment:

Now, therefore, be it Resolved, That the Senate—

(1) designates June 2015 as ``National Post-Traumatic Stress Disorder Awareness Month" and June 27, 2015, as ``National Post-Traumatic Stress Disorder Awareness Day";

(2)supports the efforts of the Secretary of Veterans

Affairs and the Secretary of Defense—as well as the entire medical community—to educate members of the Armed Forces, veterans, the families of members of the Armed Forces and veterans, and the public about the causes, symptoms, and treatment of PTSD.

(3)encourages commanders of the Armed Forces to support appropriate treatment of men and women of the Armed Forces who are diagnosed with PTSD; and

(4)respectfully requests that the Secretary of the Senate transmit a copy of this resolution to the Secretary of Veterans Affairs and the Secretary of Defense.

## II. Americans Honoring Americans

"Stamp Out PTSD" will build morale for Veterans and future recruits. When they hear the news stories about this project and when they visit the post office to buy stamps, they will feel honored. This will show America is being proactive in correcting the problems they are facing today. When we show we take care of our own, more people will step up to serve our country.

The following information further explains the need to immediately address the issue of Post-Traumatic Stress for our Veterans and for our nation:

The American Psychiatric Association defines Post Traumatic Stress Disorder (PTSD) as an anxiety problem that can manifest in some individuals after they experience extremely traumatic events, such as combat, crime, an accident, or natural disaster. PTSD was officially recognized as disorder with specific symptoms & was added to the American Psychiatric Association's Diagnostic and Statistical Manual of Mental Disorders in 1980 (1).

It is estimated that approximately 7-8% of the population will suffer from PTSD at some point in their lives, but these rates among veterans are significantly higher. Approximately 30% of men and women who have spent time in a war zone develop PTSD (2). These numbers break down even further based on the conflict.

According to the Department of Veteran Affairs:

•About 11-20 out of every 100 Veterans (or between 11-20%) who served in Operation Iraqi Freedom and Enduring Freedom have PTSD in a given year.

•About 12 out of every 100 Gulf War Veterans (or 12%) have PTSD in a given year.

•About 15 out of every 100 Vietnam Veterans (or 15%) were currently diagnosed with PTSD at the time of the most recent study in the late 1980s, the National Vietnam Veterans Readjustment Study (NVVRS). It is estimated that about 30 out of every 100 (or 30%) of Vietnam Veterans have had PTSD in their lifetime (3).

## Societal Costs of PTSD

The costs associated with PTSD are dramatic. The Congressional Budget Office estimates that treating combat veterans with PTSD was much higher than recent non-combat veterans. They place first year treatment costs at a conservative $8,000 dollars a year per case (4). The RAND Corporation estimates are higher. They estimate that cost of PTSD and major depression for two years after deployment range from $5,900 to $25,760 per case.

When applied to the totality of servicemen and women who are currently suffering from PTSD, the costs associated with its diagnoses are placed between 4-6.2 billion dollars a year (5). The United States Labor Department estimates that over 20% of Iraq and Afghanistan War Veterans are unemployed and PTSD is often cited as a contributing factor. And according to a 2011 study by HUD and the VA, upwards of 76,000 veterans will be homeless on any given night (6). And these conditions are often based on the lingering effects of PTSD.

# Suicide and PTSD

The United States faces a crisis among Veterans committing suicide. In 2013, the VA released the results of a study tracking suicide rates among Veterans from 1999 to 2010. They estimate approximately 22 veterans commit suicide each day (7).

That is nearly double the rate of suicide found among the civilian population. The National Institute of Health states that trauma survivors are 6 times more likely to commit suicide. There is a correlation between trauma and suicide and the VA identifies PTSD as a risk factor for suicide.

The VA states that one out of every 5 suicides are committed by a veteran (8). For the first time in our nation's history, military suicides now outnumber combat deaths.

REFERENCES

1. http://www.apa.org/topics/ptsd/
2. http://www.ptsd.va.gov/professional/PTSD-overview/ptsd-overview.asp
3. http://www.ptsd.va.gov/public/PTSD-overview/basics/how-common-is-ptsd.asp
4. https://www.cbo.gov/publication/42969
5. http://www.rand.org/pubs/research_briefs/RB9336.html
6. http://portal.hud.gov/hudportal/HUD?src=/press/press_releas es_media_advisories/2011/HUDNo. 11-014
7. http://www.va.gov/opa/pressrel/pressrelease.cfm?id=2427
8. http://www.publichealth.va.gov/epidemiology/studies/suicide-risk-death-risk-recent-veterans.as

## III. Allowing Everyone to Serve

We, The People want to support our Veterans. "Stamp Out PTSD" allows any citizen the opportunity to support those who serve in their own small way. This will display unity in America! That betters the human welfare of our Veterans, our citizens and it also improves the reputation of the United States in the eyes of the world.

"Stamp Out PTSD" will ignite a new trend of patriotism in a nation where no one feels that their voice can be heard. Think about how we got here to make this proposal, because of one tenacious American who wouldn't be silenced – Garland Denny.

Americans are looking to embrace positive things - we want to correct the issues important to us. Dad would say, "People will work together, this is not about Democrats or Republicans; this is about Veterans!"

He believed Americans would be excited to make a difference for Veterans! He believed it because he spent a lot of his time talking to others about his effort and their loved ones who serve.

He had the ear of the people and all of them would say that more needs to be done for our Veterans! In the supporting documents I provided a portion of the correspondence Garland received from his website that will back this up. Millions of Americans will buy this stamp. They will tell the story of how it came about, and they will write more letters to show their support. Americans want to make a difference for the people who sacrifice so much for our Freedom. My father believed in that with all his heart & soul.

# Broad National Appeal & The Public Interest

The letters, resolutions and proclamations Garland collected will demonstrate that supporting our nation's Veterans with a "Stamp Out PTSD" Semi-postal has broad national appeal, and that providing Veterans the benefit from this proposal is definitely in the national public interest.

When Garland started this effort, his main concern was that the men and women returning home from conflicts abroad were going to have needs in the future that the VA system simply wasn't even prepared to handle today. He knew we had to think ahead in order to solve the problem.

Here is a link to a video of him explaining the project around the time he started in downtown Charlotte:
https://www.youtube.com/watch?v=jJsI2lthjuw

Garland worked tirelessly to gain support for this stamp from Members of Congress, The White House, The VFW & The American Legion; he received Proclamations of support from many American towns, numerous Governors have written letters of support & thousands of people signed his petition online and in person before he passed away October 13, 2015, at the age of 84.

He was a true American Patriot who loved his country, especially Veterans! Everyone he encountered said this was a fantastic idea and that they would love to support the stamp. This is a great American story of one man's pure will to fight for what is right for the people who serve: all while dealing with struggles of his very own.

This picture was taken in Arlington National Cemetery on June 6, 2014. It was Garland's 83rd Birthday. He wanted to stop by and pay his respects.

Later that morning we met with White House Officials to discuss their support of the stamp. It was a big day for him, he told me he knew he would probably never make it back to Washington, D.C. again.

## Other Considerations

Garland would ask that you approve and implement this proposal to "Stamp Out PTSD" for our Veterans immediately. If he were here today, he would also request that you take appropriate measures to ensure "Stamp Out PTSD" has the opportunity to continue longer than the 2-year term that has been designated in the new Semi-postal rules.

This is a picture of my father and I working at a booth at the Warrior & Warbirds Air Show in Monroe, NC on Veterans Day in 2008.

Garland stood on the tarmac and talked to people over loud airplanes and got them to sign his petition. He even rallied the Boy Scouts and asked them to pass out his info.

## A Voice for the Stamp!

As we were studying the Breast Cancer Stamp, one of the things we discovered was that there should be more of a central voice behind the effort. The Postal Service will be responsible for selling these stamps, but you will have a limited budget & voice to market to the stamp over time. There will be a huge demand at first because of the media attention but how do we ensure sales will continue after the dust clears?

That is where we can help! The Denny family would like to stay involved with this project as the voice of the stamp. Our Foundation, The American Veteran Foundation, would hope to work together with the Postal Service and the VA to share stories with the public about how the stamp is impacting Veterans.

We would run the website, StampOutPTSD.com and we would cover the project using social media, tying it all into awareness for PTSD. If we share the stories of how the money is being used to make solutions, we will sell more stamps because people want to help!

We do not expect any compensation from the Postal Service or the VA for our efforts in marketing the stamp. We want to help see that this project is successful, and our family wants to continue to "Put Veterans First" into the future.

Our foundation website address is:
http://www.theamericanveteranfoundation.org

*Garland and Margaret Anne Denny*

# In Closing

There are not many men like Garland Denny. I am not saying that because he was my father, I am saying that because of his true character. He stayed dedicated to this project through thick and thin. He really felt the need to stand up for Veterans no matter what he was going through.

A few years into this, my mother's health deteriorated because of Alzheimer's. Dad cared for her at home and continued working to help Veterans. In 2009, he suffered a heart attack and had to have serious heart surgery. He had a triple bypass along with a heart valve replacement. He passed away before the procedure but was thankfully resuscitated.

The even crazier part is that there were complications after the first surgery, and he had another open-heart procedure (2 total) within 24 hours. He said the Lord spoke to him during that ordeal and he said GOD told him everything would be all right. He took it as a sign to continue caring for my mother and his mission for Veterans. He worked to regain his strength and he pushed forward.

Mom got to a point where she relied heavily on dad. He would set his alarm & check on her throughout the night. He wouldn't let himself sleep more than an hour at a time without getting up to make sure she was okay. When the sun came up, he would start his phone calls for Vets.

After mom passed away in 2013, you could tell a part of his heart was missing. He was married to her for 59 years and he loved her dearly. He became weaker as time moved on, and his nose would run constantly. In the picture below, you can see his cane in one hand and his handkerchief in the other. His voice got softer and softer by the day. I used to joke with him that it was because he talked so much during his 84 years. He laughed and told me "I have been a very fortunate man".

Dad was always determined to accomplish this goal. In this picture along with failing health, his focus was always on working for our veterans. Whenever I walked beside him, I felt like I had to put my arm behind him. He never really needed my support, but I guess in some way I just wanted him to know I was behind him.

He continues to lead the way today & I am still behind him working to see veterans get what he thought they deserved. In a letter you will read below, Congress suggested we have a national showing of support to help make Stamp-Out PTSD for Veterans an enormous success! My question is, will you stand behind Garland as well?

Thank you for allowing me to opportunity to share Garland Denny's Stamp Out PTSD proposal to help Veterans. If it were not for HIS hard work and sheer determination to help Veterans, I would not be communicating with you today.

May GOD Bless our Troops and these United States of America!

# PROCLAMATION

| | |
|---|---|
| Whereas: | The nation is blessed with men and women who voluntarily swear an oath to defend the Constitution of the United States of America against all enemies, foreign and domestic; and |
| Whereas: | These men and women make great personal sacrifices in the name of our Constitution thereby ensuring the perpetuation of our individual liberties; and |
| Whereas: | These same men and women voluntarily make great personal sacrifices to carry democracy and extend the freedoms we enjoy to the underprivileged of the world; and |
| Whereas: | Some of these men and women will incur great personal hardships and catastrophic injury in the performance of their duties; and |
| Whereas: | We feel duty bound to honor, support, and provide relief to these warriors and their families; NOW |
| Therefore, | I, Thomas M. Menino, Mayor of the City of Boston, do hereby unequivocally support the initiative of implementing a new government bond, stamp and coin program, the proceeds from which shall be used exclusively for those warriors and their families who have borne the brunt of preserving our freedoms and extending those freedoms throughout the world. |

Mayor

X-7130 

# IMPATIENTLY WAITING

While we were waiting for the USPS to change their rules, all we could do was wait. I don't have the patience to wait for anything, so I continued doing what dad taught me to do, which was politickin'. It was 2016, an election year, a big one mind you because there was a race for the Presidency.

Hillary Clinton was running against Donald Trump and social media was in a frenzy over the ordeal, it still is today as you are reading this book. Anyway, the election brings all the big names to town, and dad had prepared me to carry on his advocating. I knew that any time I could get in front of the leaders or potential new leaders it would help our cause.

Looking back, it was amazing that I was able to insert myself into the lives of some of the most powerful political people in our country. Some of that was of my own making, other times I had a little help from friends who serve veterans. Let me tell you about the fun I had, hopefully it will inspire you to start reaching out to future leaders right from your home.

In March of 2016, I saw a newspaper article that said former President Bill Clinton was coming to speak at Johnson C. Smith University in Charlotte. You didn't need a ticket to see him speak and no donation was expected like it is these days. This was my first time going out to politickin' on my own. I got up that morning and put on my suit and drove down to the college.

My plan was to always arrive at these events early, and I had a few things with me each time. I carried a short letter that would explain what we were doing for Veterans, and it was placed in an unsealed envelope. That made the Secret Service agents feel better. I also carried dad's book of 4x6 pictures that would show him with: President Clinton, President Carter, General Wesley Clark, Senator Elizabeth Dole, Congressman Robert Pittenger, and many others. Dad had an impressive photo collection that I can quickly flip through in a moment or two.

I took this picture of President Clinton speaking at JCSU; there seemed to be about a thousand people out there under that pretty clock tower listening to what he had to say. He was there stumping for his wife Hillary.

After his speech was over, he went to shaking hands with the people closest to the stage. I was one of those people and it would be my first chance to promote the Veterans Petition without my father by my side. I got the chance to tell him that we had met with him back in March of 2008 at the VFW which was not too far away from this location. I pulled out the group of pictures and he was pleasantly surprised. I handed him that unsealed envelope and I asked him to review it quickly before he left the location and he said that he would and asked me to stick around a while.

After he was done meeting with people, he looked over to me and held up a finger, no, not the middle one, this was the sign to wait one moment. He went into a building on campus, many attendees had given his aides things to sign. Some of them had pictures, others had books. After a little bit of time, the president walked back out and quickly spoke to me, he said I want you to know I am going to share this with people and then he handed me a back a portion of the letter I wrote him. He had torn off a piece and he signed his name.

It doesn't matter if you care for his political ideology or not, not many people get to meet a President once, this was my second time. Walking back to my car, I knew my dad was with me in spirit. I was proud of myself for going alone and taking a chance to carry this mission on, it was a melancholy experience that taught me to stay focused.

# A BEER

Letters are still an effective way of communicating. Here is another letter that I wrote to President Obama where I asked him to have a beer with me. Once again, the president responded to me, and I wanted to share the complete exchange with you.

You'll see my handwritten letter that I mailed to the White House using a Breast Cancer Awareness Stamp. That raised funds for Breast Cancer Awareness.

When the president mailed me back, my postman Jeremy was kind enough to leave it at my door. He told me later that he didn't want to have to bend it to fit inside my mailbox. Thank you, Jeremy!

Now, for the record, I wrote President Trump's team similar letters as well. I always kept a copy of what I sent too. Remember, this is not about our favorite Democrats or Republicans. This is about our VETERANS!

That is a key concept in taking this program even further than it has already come. Together, we can ensure these programs continue indefinitely and that will encourage those out there who are suffering from PTSD to seek the help they need. It will help them see that they are not alone. Americans care!

1 of 2

3-16-2016

Dear Mr. President,

I wanted to take just a minute to tell you that I appreciate the work you have done as our President. You have done some great things for America and I definetly feel as if my lifes situation has improved during your time in office. Thank you for all of your hard work!

I have written you many times, I normally send emails but this time I wanted to go with an old school letter. I wanted to support Breast Cancer and I also wanted to make a request to you. Who am I kidding? I am just trying to invite myself over to your place for a beer, some of that White House Beer. I heard it was pretty good and I thought it would be cool to sit down with you on the South Lawn and look out over Washington.

I want to be 100% honest with you, I dont want to talk about politics it is understandable that this should not be on America's time, so I don't mind the evenings or the weekends. You let me know what works and I will be there!

You are probably thinking "if this guy doesn't want to talk politics, what does he want to talk about?" I really just want to get some advice from you.

I want to know what you think we could do to help more Veterans in the future. After you leave office I will continue to fight (as I have done) for them and what is right - so that their situation always improves.

What do you think? You got time for a cold one? Thank you Mr. President!

"Let's Put Veterans First"

Regards,

Chuck Denny
2301 Genesis Drive
Monroe, NC 28110
980-721-2663

THE WHITE HOUSE
WASHINGTON

August 22, 2016

Mr. Chuck Denny
Monroe, North Carolina

Dear Chuck:

Thanks for the great letter, and for writing to me over the past few years.

While your offer to grab a beer and talk anything but politics is a thoughtful one, I'll be busy working to bring about every last bit of change I can during the fourth quarter of my Presidency. And that includes looking out for our veterans. Since my first days in Office my Administration has been working to make sure those who have fought for our freedom don't have to fight to take part in our country's promise, and I am grateful for your dedication to that mission as well. As you continue giving back to those who have given so much for us, I encourage you to keep leading by example and striving to make a difference in your community—you'll help change lives for the better and inspire others to join in this important work along the way.

Thanks again for reaching out to me. If more people pursue progress with the kind of good humor and optimism that came across in your message, I know there is nothing our country can't achieve. Keep at it—and know I'll be standing right alongside you, doing the same.

Sincerely,

Hey there Mr. President, in case you happen to be reading this, my offer still stands!

# MY TRUMP CARDS

After I was able to meet with President Clinton on my own, I embarked on a whirlwind political tour. If someone was coming to town to stump for a candidate, I put my personal life on hold to try and meet with them. Democrat or Republican. I would wait patiently for many long hours just to have a few critical moments to discuss the needs of our veterans. Good people need our help, folk who are suffering because they served America and that needed to change. It still does.

I tried my hardest to reach President Trump before and after he was elected to office. A lot of people tried to help me score a meeting with him as well. I wrote letters, I sent emails, I made phone calls and when that was ineffective, I started having my friends, family, veterans and veteran organizations make the same request. We had to meet with both sides of the aisle to serve our Veterans well.

I have a copy of a letter I wrote to President Trump that dates to June 11, 2008. I sent it to the Trump Organization in New York. If you look at the Presidential records from the time he was elected in office, I made hundreds of calls to the White House.

Ultimately, I was able to meet in person with some of the highest-ranking members of President Trump's most inner circle and even his family too, you will see. Now, I am not saying at all that President Trump didn't serve the needs of our veterans. I'm not pouting or calling him names. If you look to the National Archives, you should see the letters I wrote him were addressed as "Honorable President Donald Trump". (Unless they happen to be in Joe Biden's Garage). Sorry, I couldn't resist.

President Trump, if you happen to be reading this, I want you to know I'm not mad at you sir, and I hope you consider this book as my new request to meet with you IMMEDIATELY to talk about helping our Veterans. And to formally address a plan to Help Heal PTSD far into the future. We still have time to do some magnificent things!

It's important to note that President Trump has done some great things for many Veterans. I'm not trying to take any of that away from him. I'm saying I want my fair shot to speak directly with him about Garland Denny and this effort to help veterans. It's proven to be a worthy cause; a lot of Americans have joined the mission; and President Trump should be included. It's my opinion that he missed a huge opportunity to be a part of a solution if you ask me!

*Chuck Denny with Ivanka Trump*

Two days before the election of 2016, I saw that Ivanka Trump was coming to my little town in North Carolina. At the time, I was living in Indian Trail, and she was coming to speak with a group of Republicans. I just knew that this was going to be my best chance at reaching her father to discuss our grass roots efforts to help Veterans.

As you can see, I came up a little short standing beside Ivanka, but I completed my goal which was to meet with her, speak with her a few moments and present her with some information that she could pass to her father and then grab a picture of us together so I could prove I did what I could to push this forward for our veterans. I knew President Trump was going to win the election that year and I thought for sure I would hear back from someone from his staff with big news.

This is a picture that I snapped of Ivanka's staffers that were traveling with her that day, I don't know their names but the dark-haired lady on the right of the picture is holding my huge unsealed manilla envelope of information about the stamp project.

I love how she's staring directly at me when I took this photo. I can't help but wonder if she has purchased some of the 18 million stamps to help veterans that have already been sold as of today.

It's a good question, don't you think?

When her father was elected to office I amped up my efforts to meet with him. By this time, I had spoken with President Clinton, Hillary Clinton, Congressman Pittenger, and quite a few other members of Congress. I was even able to talk with Bowzer of Sha-Na-Na. I was sure in my mind that someone from President Trump's staff was going to reach out to me at any time.

A few months went by after the election and then I got an invitation to meet the Speaker of the House Kevin McCarthy when he was in Charlotte, speaking at The Duke Mansion. How cool is that?

*Chuck Denny with the Speaker of the House Kevin McCarthy*

I was slowly but surely communicating directly with some of the most powerful people in our nation. I am thankful for everyone who made these memories happen and the effort that was put into making changes for Veterans. I was still on a mission to meet directly with President Trump, and I asked the speaker to talk with the president about helping me score a meeting with him, but I never spoke with him or any member of his staff again after that day. One can't say that I didn't try.

Then there was a time I got word that a close ally of President Trump's team was coming to town to speak with a group of REALTORS® about policy. I have been a REALTOR® since 1998, I figured that this would be another great chance to hear what the man had to say and to put a packet of information in his hands with the hopes that he would speak with the president about our efforts to help veterans.

His name was Mick Mulvaney, he was a former House Representative from South Carolina and at the time I saw him speak, he was serving America as the Director of the Office of Management and Budget from February 2017 until sometime in 2020. This picture was taken in 2018.

*Chuck Denny with Mick Mulvaney*

Once again, I just knew we had another great shot at scoring a meeting with the president to talk about healing PTSD. I was able to speak with him a few moments and point out that this was a perfect chance for him to tell the president that this effort would help our Veterans without increasing taxes or the national deficit. I felt like that was a relevant point he could make to explore a direct conversation with the president, hopefully the next time they met. He went on to become President Trump's Chief of Staff and I had never heard from him again.

As time progressed, I didn't understand for the life of me why the current administration wouldn't help set up a meeting with me to discuss the project. We had made tremendous progress and if the president would get direct word of this, I knew he would help, and this project would skyrocket.

I saw first-hand that President Trump cared for our veterans, I knew he wanted to be creative and help improve matters where he could, this was the perfect opportunity. Why was it so hard to score a formal meeting with him or a high-ranking member of his staff? We had all this proof that veterans and citizens were behind us; doing what was right for our heroes. I'm still having a hard time trying to figure that out to this day.

I told you earlier that I went on a whirlwind political tour and the fun didn't stop there. I saw on a local news segment that Vice President Pence was coming to speak in town. It was again another perfect opportunity for me to stump for veterans while the politicians were just looking for more constituents.

I was this close to a conversation with President Trump's right-hand man in April of 2018. I didn't get the chance to speak directly to VP Pence about helping our veterans, but his aide got my open letter. I am good with that if that staffer was kind enough to pass the VP the information that I handed him.

*Vice President Pence*

In that picture, a veteran's wife and community advocate got the chance to share her thoughts with Mr. Pence. Her husband was a disabled veteran who was sitting in his wheelchair, Vice President Pence is focused on speaking with him. This event proves at least 5 high-ranking people in government knew we were working to Help Heal PTSD. I couldn't wait for the chance to speak with them.

July 11, 2008

The Trump Organization
Attn: Mr. Donald Trump
725 Fifth Avenue
New York, NY 10022

Re: Urgent - Time Sensitive - Our Petition to Congress to help Veterans!

Dear Mr. Trump,

We would like to ask for your help (non-monetary) in petitioning Congress to create a new Bill. This Bill could be passed into law by our next President on 1-21-2009. This Law will benefit EVERY VETERAN and their immediate family.

**Why should this be done?**
Many soldiers have paid the ultimate price for us to enjoy our Freedom. Throughout time, soldiers have returned home to encounter hardships; physically, emotionally, medically, financially, and psychologically. None of these men and women should have to wait on politics for care or financial assistance, but unfortunately, that is what is happening. There are existing programs out there but they are behind in the times.

**Here is what we are thinking:**
The new law would allow the government to sell coins, stamps and bonds to the public. We are asking in the petition to honor "The Tomb of the Unknowns". The profit or surcharge generated from the sale of these coins, stamps and bonds will go straight to helping Veterans and their families in need. This money would be used to provide new shelters, improved medical facilities, medical assistance, prescription assistance and even monetary support for those families who have lost loved ones that paid the ultimate sacrifice to protect the Freedom of every American.

**How you can help:**
We need over 60,000 people to sign this petition so Congress will listen to us. Please sign the Veterans Petition online @ www.veteranspetition.com . Then write your Representatives and Congressional Leaders and ask them to support this effort immediately.

Together, we can show all Veterans past, present and future that we appreciate what they have done for us as individuals and as a country. Let's fight for them this time to provide them with better medical care, better medical benefits, more medical and physical care facilities, prompt financial assistance and a chance for economical housing.

Garland B. Denny
Charles K. Denny
980-721-2663 - direct

# THE AMERICAN VETERAN FOUNDATION

624 Matthews-Mint Hill Road · Suite 117
Matthews, North Carolina 28105

**WWW.HELPFIGHTPTSD.COM**

**PHONE: 980-721-2663**

1.25.17

Dear President Trump,

Congratulations on becoming the 45th President of the United States of America. I am writing you today to ask you to focus on helping Veterans living with Post Traumatic Stress.

It would be GREAT to bring together the smartest minds in America (at the White House) to focus on our Veterans who live with this problem daily. We need to take better care of our own sir and there is an opportunity to offer some help without increasing taxes or the national debt.

Congressman Robert Pittenger (NC-09) and 127 other members of Congress support this effort to help Veterans President Trump. I would love the chance to meet with you and the Congressman at the White House to discuss a strategy moving forward.

Taking our time to identify & address the medical needs of those who volunteer to serve is not only in our national public interest President Trump, it should be our highest national priority. I honestly believe that America will unite together and work for Veterans. I have personally seen the passion and love America holds for our men and women in uniform.

May God Bless Our Troops and these United States of America.

Regards,

Chuck Denny
Founder

# THE ALZHEIMER'S STAMP

So, here is the cliff notes version of how things progressed. Dad passed away and I wrote that letter to the US Postmaster General on December 1, 2015, that pointed her to the congressional letter of support. The following January, the US Postmaster General detailed in the Federal Register that they intended to change some of the rules with regards to the semi-postal program. It took them 4 months to implement the changes but when they did, it opened the door for anyone to make a submission for a new discretionary semi-postal stamp. That was what Ms. Mary-Ann Penner explained in her letter to me.

So, from this point, I started working frantically on the submission. You know the saying GOD works in mysterious ways; well, we are about to see another instance of that in this chapter. If you remember back to the Veterans Petition chapter, I put a short paragraph in there that explained my mother passed away from complications from Alzheimer's. And then in the submission, you learned a little bit more about how dad took care of mom while he was making this happen.

To make a long story a little shorter, after a certain time period of receiving first round submissions for new Discretionary semi-postals, it was announced by the US Postmaster General, Meghan Brennan that the Alzheimer's stamp would be released in 2017 and also that the Healing PTSD stamp would be released in 2019. They would be called Discretionary Semi-Postal Stamps, and they would only be available for a limited time.

Dad would not have had it play out any other way. He knew a veteran's stamp was important but after living through losing his wife of 59 years, who suffered from Alzheimer's while he was working on this project, I'd say it reduces all the way down to Devine Inspiration. Looking back, it's not hard to see that a higher hand was helping all of this along.

I wrote an email to Ms. Penner and asked her to pass a message along to the Postmaster General, thanking her for her compassion and the tough decision she had to make. She had no idea our family was impacted by Alzheimer's, but it was definitely the right decision to make.

The Postmaster General then invited me up to the Alzheimer's Stamp public release. It was held at John Hopkin's University, and I got to sit in the front row with the family that made that submission. It was a great day for Alzheimer's patients and their families, and it was another proud moment for me. There were many people who made these moments possible, and I smile every time I think about my trip alone up to Baltimore in November of 2017. It was exciting to see how the USPS was going to roll it out.

*Chuck Denny pictured with US Postmaster General Meghan Brennan*

# NO POLITICS – JUST PATRIOTISM

In March of 2017, I was sitting in my office in Matthews, North Carolina trying to figure out how to bring people together to push the stamp program forward. Out of nowhere, it hit me like a lightning bolt. Usually, the Sunday before Memorial Day, there is a big racing event at the speedway and if you've ever attended its hard as hell to walk away from that place and not feel proud to be an American.

It's a 600-mile race around a 1.5-mile track. That is 400 laps and man are there some sights to see. There are skydivers, military planes, loud race cars, lots of beer and chicken wings. Thousands of veterans and everyday citizens are sitting in the stands, and some are watching from the tops of their campers in the infield. It's normally a day where everyone attending will be honoring all of those that gave their lives for our freedom. They put on an event like nobody else; back in the 1990's that place would pack in close to 170,000 people.

I thought to myself, how cool would it be if I put together an event and gave people the chance to show some solidarity for our veterans too? I wanted to do it differently though. I wanted this event to be absolutely, 100% free and I didn't want to hear or see a dang thing about politics.

Anyway, you should always begin with the end in mind and my idea was to organize a ride. I used Facebook to post an event called the "No Politics – Just Patriotism Ride." If you didn't know it, around the city of Charlotte, we have a bypass that is a 65-mile loop. It allows you to miss a lot of the traffic when you don't want to drive through the city.

Early on Sunday mornings, it's not too crowded so I knew it would be perfect for our needs and a hell of a lot safer than that racetrack, lol. I got the idea from a thought I had about the upcoming race and the movie Convoy. I scheduled it on my calendar for the Sunday before Memorial Day and I knew it was going to happen come hell or high water.

I closed my eyes and envisioned myself driving that loop like I have done many times. The main goal was for veterans and their families to feel the love from and for America. The second goal was for all the participants to walk away feeling proud that they played a part in reaching our main goal. I took a good hard look directly into the future that day, and I used Garland's formula of making sure that EVERYONE would have a chance to participate even in the smallest way. I realized there may be some folk who may not be able to make the drive and I wanted everyone to know the USA needed them this day, so I started planting some seeds.

I went down and spoke to Charlotte Mayor Jennifer Roberts and told her what I was planning. She liked the idea and wanted to show Charlotte supported the effort, so she wrote a proclamation that declared the day of the event, Garland B. Denny Day.

*Chuck Denny with Charlotte Mayor Jennifer Roberts*

Next, I reached out to the Charlotte Fire Department in downtown Charlotte, and I told them what I was planning, and I asked the Chief if he could do a favor for me. I told him that we could work together to honor veterans by having as many Firetrucks as possible positioned on each overpass along the bypass and they could display a large American Flag. He told me it was a great symbol of Freedom and since the bypass runs through many little towns, I should reach out to their Fire Captains and ask for their support too. So, I did it.

Then I reached out to the Chief of Police's office for the City of Charlotte. I told them the plan and asked for their support. I explained this day was about nothing more than our veterans and it would be great if the Police could lead the convoy. I mentioned there would be motorcycles, trucks, vintage cars, jeeps, and everyday vehicles too.

We couldn't work out a deal with the Charlotte Police department. They didn't like the visual message that we would be sending so they impolitely declined my offer. That suited me just fine because this wasn't about politics and boy were they playing the political card right out of the gate. I still have nothing but love for the Charlotte Police, I have friends who are serving on the force now, that is no shot to them. It's just how it all happened. So, I reached out to the Matthews Police Department, and they were graciously eager to serve our needs in the ways they could within their policy.

Next, I knew the town of Matthews had just finished their Sportsplex right down the street from my office. It wasn't even open to the public yet, so I reached out to the director of the facility. I explained the event and told him it would be a perfect staging area for our starting point. It could accommodate all the vehicles that would show up and plus the Matthews Police would be there to help us direct traffic all the way out to the bypass. He agreed to let us use the parking lots as well as the PA system, and things sure were starting to fall into place.

Then I got the idea to reach out to the Carolina Panthers. I told them what we're doing down in Matthews, and since they had helped us spread the word about the Veterans Petition, I knew they would help. I invited Sir Purr and the Panther Cheerleaders down to come meet with all the attendees. People loved it, they had the perfect chance to serve veterans and get some very cool photos of all the day's events.

Over the years, we picked up a lot of support from our local radio personalities. John Hancock over at WBT radio allowed me to call into his show and tell his listeners about this event for free a couple of different times. So did John Boy and Billy over at the Fox. Shane and the team at WIXE in Monroe interviewed us a few times over the years too. The radio personalities around the Queen City and their entire teams are some of the biggest radio personalities around the country and some of the nicest folks you could ever meet.

Ace and TJ are in the same category, just a little more conservative at heart. Those fellas at Kiss helped us promote the event too, but they made me pay $1000 for like six 1-minute segments over 5 days. Sorry to throw you under the bus guys, it's just the truth. Readers, you shouldn't be mad at them for charging us, because they do a lot for our community too. Especially kids. I am just razzing them a little bit here with my pen. I have nothing but love for them and you should too, their tagline is "If you grin, you're in." Love you Ace and TJ, I mean it, for real!

As these situations started compiling, I would post the progress on the event page on social media, and I continued to drop ideas about how people could join us. Since the Fire Department was going to be posted up on most of the bridges, I told people who planned to attend to invite their friends and family to come out and support us too. They could stand on the bridges and wave their flags as our convoy drove 65 miles.

After a lot of hard work, the day finally arrived. But before I tell you any more about this, I have to say a few things. I had tons of help from my family, friends, and the community. I am thankful for the Police and Fireman who offered their help. The VFW #5464 along with their Ladies Auxiliary in Monroe was instrumental in spreading the word. Biker club members and Car club members did their part to show us love. We had a few politicians show up to work with us and many other citizens that I didn't personally know too.

So many folks pitched in, and we were all proud of this great country we live in! This day would not have been possible without the many selfless AMERICANS who did their small part to help us reach the goals that I originally set for the event. Our country needs more of this comradery and brotherhood to bring us closer together. One thing is for sure, we were all excited about the day and what was to come, and we couldn't wait to see how things were going to pan out.

My family and I got to the Sportsplex early that morning. The Matthews Fire Department rolled in and positioned themselves at our dedicated starting point. They extended the ladder as high as it would go and then angled it perfectly over the road so that every person would roll underneath the cover of Old Glory as we started our drive around the city. It was a beautiful sight to see.

Bikers started rolling in, cool classic cars too. There were Jeeps, big GMC trucks, Mini-Vans, little Ford trucks, Corvettes, Mercedes, and hell I think a fiat showed up too. People came in full force, flags were flying from just about every vehicle, people had on their patriotic gear. You could feel the love for America, you could see and hear it too.

*Photo Courtesy of Mr. Vincent Blake, Veteran*

As we got closer and closer to the event's start time, that parking area got more and more crowded. We had a playlist of good American music playing over the public address system. A huge flag flew on the Videotron. People were hanging out and touring all the cars and introducing themselves to each other. It was a great way to honor all those who gave their life for our country.

When things got started, we said the Pledge of Allegiance together, and then dad's preacher, Rev. Tom Gillespie, prayed over the attendees and asked GOD to keep us safe as we honored our veterans. He left his congregation that Sunday morning just to come share this moment with us all. We call each other brothers to this day, and I know exactly why my father loved and trusted him.

*William Stinson Jr, George White, Rev. Thomas Gillespie & John White*

One of my childhood buddies John White drove all the way down from Kettering, Ohio, to attend with other members of his family. He played Taps on his trumpet to honor the fallen, and then we held a moment of silence, it was a beautiful sequence of events.

Eventually, the roar of motorcycles filled the air and thousands of people geared up to embark on our journey around the town. It was a very impressive site to see. And a true honor to be a part of, if you do some looking on our Facebook Page, The American Veteran Foundation, you will see the videos Matthews Mayor Jim Taylor filmed of our procession as we all rolled out under old glory. I also included the links at the end of this chapter. Police were directing us to the interstate, and it was one wild and crazy ride. There were people standing on bridges waving to the procession, and flags were flying everywhere.

I had even reached out to the White House for a few months straight and asked President Trump to fly in front of us on Air Force One. That would have been the ultimate symbol of solidarity if you asked me. He had other commitments that day but I'm glad everyone was kept safe; it turned out to be an awesome day.

When the ride was over many of the folks who participated returned back to the Sportsplex to reflect on the event. Seeing the smiles and the happiness for myself, I could tell it filled a missing void in our country these days. It left us all hungry, wanting others to feel a deeper love for America, so to speak.

Hopefully, we will do it again sometime soon in the future and you can join us too, what do you think?

Here are links to two videos of the event posted by Mayor Jim Taylor of Matthews:

https://www.facebook.com/MayorJimTaylor/videos/1372943082790424

https://www.facebook.com/MayorJimTaylor/videos/1372944882790244

# DAD'S DREAM ON DISPLAY

The power of the mind is a wonderful thing. Within ourselves, we all can create a vision and with a little tenacity, that thought can be seen to fruition. The hardest part is keeping your faith in believing the dream can be accomplished. The second hardest part is the time constraint from beginning to end. We live in a world where instant gratification and impatience thrive, that hinders our abilities to see something through when it could take a long period of time.

The Healing PTSD "Discretionary" Semi-postal Stamp was issued December 2, 2019, in Charlotte, NC. That vision was 12 years in the making, to put that into perspective that is 4,380 days. You know the old saying, "Rome wasn't built in a day."

I remember early in October of 2018 that I got a telephone call from a (202) area code, I knew it was from D.C... I picked up the call and a man named Michael Henry told me he was with the USPS. He was calling to tell me he would be working on organizing the event to release the Healing PTSD stamp to the public and that it would be held in Charlotte, in December the following year.

He went on to explain that since our foundation was instrumental in creating the stamp, he would like my input on a location for the event and putting together a launch. He told me that he would be reaching back out to me again in January with more information. So, once again I was patiently waiting for the wizard to appear.

About 18 days into the new year, Mr. Henry called to shore up some of their plans and right before the call ended, I asked him to do me a favor. I told him the rednecks around here don't tend to believe much that flies from the lips, so if he could, it would be nice to put what we spoke about in writing. That way I would have proof in ink when I started spreading the word. It is smart to always get it in writing if you know what I mean. He laughed a little bit and obliged my request, and I received his letter on January 23, 2019.

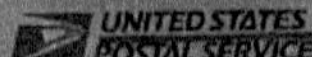 UNITED STATES
POSTAL SERVICE

January 23, 2019

Mr. Chuck Denny
2035 Applebrook Drive
Monroe, NC 28110


Dear Mr. Denny,

This letter confirms the United States Postal Service's interest in holding a First Day of Issue Stamp Ceremony for the Post Traumatic Stress Disorder semi-postal stamp at the forum you are planning in Charlotte, North Carolina the first week of December 2019.

The Postal Service holds a First Day of Issue Ceremony whenever a new stamp is released. A typical ceremony consists of the Presentation of Colors, singing of the National Anthem, a dedication of the stamp by an USPS officer, the unveiling of the stamp, and remarks from people associated with the stamp's subject. The new stamp is sold on site at the ceremony, as well as in post offices across the USA for the first time that day.

Thank you for your support and efforts on behalf of those suffering from PTSD. We look forward to working with you on the event in December and thank you for including the USPS in your plans. Please let me know if you need additional information or support at this time.

Just a reminder that the PTSD semi postal stamp has not been announced publicly. Please share this information on a need to know basis.


Respectfully,

Michael J. Henry

Stamp Development Specialist
United States Postal Service
475 L'enfant Plaza SW
Washington DC 20260
michael.j.henry@usps.gov
202.907.9032

I remember the day that I pulled it from our mailbox, it was a great sight to see. Even at that moment though, it was still hard to believe. We had been working on this for so long, I was almost numb to the thought of it occurring, because there had been many setbacks along the way. We all know working with the government brings a level of skepticism and frustration.

Not too much happened until August and September rolled around, pretty much nothing but excuses and emails. I am thankful that they made their rule changes and approved the stamp but, in my mind, this was a much bigger deal than the USPS team was making it out to be. The planning of the launch could have been way more effective in selling more stamps from the get-go. As more time passed, I could tell this was just another stamp release launch to them. They seemed to miss the point of hope and inspiration and that was what we were selling here.

To me and a lot of others, this had been almost a decade of a lot of heart and soul. To them, it was this one who gets the same attention that the others did. We were three months out from the launch, and I finally told them nobody around here believes that this will even happen anyway, many of the final details hadn't been firmed up by the team and I was told to have patience. Think about that for a minute, lol. Eventually, I got word that the USPS team was coming to town, so I was a little more relieved but perturbed at the same time. As we got closer to the event, I was glad to see their attitudes change.

Mr. Michael Henry and Mr. Artis Montgomery made a trip down to Charlotte from D.C. I was able to arrange for the three of us a meeting with the Mayor, Vi Lyles, to talk about the launch, and then we toured a few venues. One choice was the Blumenthal Performing Arts Center which is located inside the tallest skyscraper downtown. We also checked out the NASCAR Hall of Fame facility but in the end, they chose the McGlohan Theater, which is pictured here, and I was thrilled.

That is such a beautiful building, it is a renovated church that was turned into a performing arts center; located right in the heart of Charlotte. There is lots of stained glass, and it offered a very peaceful and intimate setting, it was perfect for the release.

Finally, the day had arrived, we all had been waiting for what seemed like eternity for these moments of time. The USPS had a tight itinerary set up that started around 6:30am. The ceremony started promptly at 11am and was to be finished at 2pm. We got there around 9:30 that morning to check out the sites and just to absorb the moment, to appreciate all the hard work and effort that went into making this day. At first there were mainly just USPS workers doing their setup procedures. Outside in the lobby, they were organizing tables, placing signs, and unfolding posters around the venue, others were inside setting up the stage. On that stage, there was a large banner of the stamp, it must be 12 feet tall, that became my personal memento of the day.

That place could hold 750 people and if I remember right, it was half full, but they still sold a lot of stamps. I am thankful for all of the people who wanted to be a part of that monumental feat, but I sure do wish Mayor Liles, President Trump and all the other high-ranking people would have sat with us and their staffers in that venue, but it seems like politics got into the way. Maybe it was just poor planning because I had contacted these folks about a thousand times about the event, so it had to be the short period of time between when the invitations were sent out and the actual event day. Well, it was the USPS's event and they thought it would be appropriate, what do you say?

There were a lot of great things about the event itself and ultimately it brought people together to reach our mission. We had the Wounded Warriors with us, and one of the leading researchers of PTSD in the nation, Dr. Paula Schnurr and even the Red Cross.

It was a bittersweet moment for me personally because my father wasn't there physically to see the fruit of his efforts finally pay off. He was there in spirit of course; I knew that, and I made sure that his voice would be heard so that he could play his part on that monumental day.

After my introduction speech, I pulled out my telephone and asked the audience to listen to his words. I opened a voice recording that I had made of dad before he passed away and put the recorder to the microphone. Here is what he had to say: "Unless this country comes together and tries to unite and forget about what party you are in and put our country first, I think our country is doomed. Love your neighbor and if you don't know them or have never heard of them, be kind.

And try to do something to make this a better country. Forget about this - I am right and you are wrong, or it's my way or the highway - on both sides. God bless everybody and thanks for your time."

Here is a link to a YouTube video that was released about the launch by the USPS: https://youtu.be/RvHd92XCFV4?si=YGCafGTJJEynivtZ

On his DD 214 discharge paper from the military, it lists Garland's highest grade of education was the 8th grade. Look at what he accomplished in his time on earth. Anything is possible when people join together for a good cause. We still have some more work to do to complete this project and we are hoping that you will help us.

By law, the USPS Discretionary Semi-Postal program will expire in November of 2027. This program won't continue unless we work together again to pressure Congress for their immediate attention. As you have read, there have been thousands of folks over the years who did their small part in making this dream a reality and there is still time for you to join Garland's mission to help. We need an immediate act of Congress to extend this program indefinitely; a bill signed off by all members of Congress and inked by the president sitting at the resolute desk.

Believe it or not, there are numerous instances where people have reached out to me after the roll out to tell me that their post office doesn't carry the stamps, or they didn't have any in stock or would have to order them. That has to change, and it will, but we need your help to make sure it happens.

Here are the very simple steps you can take to help make sure this project lives indefinitely. Please go to the USPS and buy a sheet of Healing PTSD stamps today. If they don't have them in the facility, order them from the USPS website.

Then handwrite 7 letters asking the recipients for their help in healing America's Heroes! Ask them to support continuing this project & provide your story why it's important. Sign each letter and address the envelope using a blue pen; write one to your member of the House, one to each of your two Senators, write one to President Joe Biden, write one to former President Donald Trump, write one to US Postmaster General Louis DeJoy and finally write to the USPS Board of Governors. I'll provide you some addresses in just a few pages. Make sure to use a Healing PTSD Stamp to cover the postage cost and point out in your letter that it is raising funds for PTSD and that won't continue without their help!

Go to the USPS in your town and have them postmark each letter with the date it was mailed, then take a quick photo of each envelope with your phone **before** they send it on its way. Make sure to keep a personal copy of your letter as well. Share them frequently on your social media and share this story with everyone you can get to listen.

Ask in each letter that the recipient immediately acknowledge **OUR** efforts to this day and pledge they will do whatever it takes to continue this program for the benefit of our veterans and all Americans who may be living with PTSD. Please make sure to tell them you are a part of Garland's army and mention respectfully that it is time for the madness in Washington, D.C. to end!

This is not about "Democrats or Republicans", this is about the future of our nation and showing the world how fast Americans will come together to take care of our own!

Thank you for buying this book and reading this story and thank you for working with us to Help Heal PTSD.

May God Bless America.

*The Denny's standing outside the West Wing.*

# www.HelpHealPTSD.com

~ 149 ~

Visit this link to see current USPS sales of the stamp:

https://about.usps.com/what/corporate-social-responsibility/activities/semipostals.htm

# CONTACT LIST

The White House
1600 Pennsylvania Ave NW
Washington, DC 20500

The Honorable (name)
US House of Representatives
Washington DC 20515

The Honorable (name)
US Senate
Washington DC 20515

Postmaster General Louis DeJoy
USPS – Headquarters
475 L'Enfant Plaza SW
Washington DC 20260-0010

Board of Governors
USPS – Headquarters
475 L'Enfant Plaza SW
Washington DC 20260-0004

Former President Trump's Website states he prefers not to receive letters and that you contact him online at:

https://www.45office.com/info/share-your-thoughts

* 9 7 9 8 3 2 4 5 5 3 9 4 4 *